Micromotives
and Macrobehavior

FELS LECTURES ON PUBLIC POLICY ANALYSIS
Sponsored by the Fels Center of
Government, the University of Pennsylvania

Micromotives
and Macrobehavior

THOMAS C. SCHELLING

W · W · NORTON & COMPANY   New York   London

Library of Congress Cataloging in Publication Data
Schelling, Thomas C   1921–
    Micromotives and macrobehavior.

    (Fels lectures on public policy analysis)
    Includes index.
    1. Policy sciences.   2. Choice (Psychology).
3. Social choice.   4. Collective behavior.   5. Social
problems.   I. Title.   II. Series.
H61.S355 1978   301.11'3   78–17119
ISBN 0–393–05701–1
ISBN 0–393–09009–4 pbk.

2 3 4 5 6 7 8 9 0

Contents

Acknowledgments

When I reflect on it I am surprised at how much of what I write, including things that please me, I write at somebody's invitation. Julius Margolis asked me to use the Fels Lectures to collect some thoughts he knew I was working on; I might have collected them anyway, but I might not, and surely not so soon. Emmanuel Mesthene urged me earlier to put on paper some thoughts he knew I was working on; they are here too, perhaps only because he did. And some parts of this book, like Chapters 2 and 7, were more years getting straightened out than you might believe; if you like them you can thank a number of people who, while contributing ideas in private and in print, were especially generous with their enthusiasm, a nourishment without which I find it hard to work. They are Graham T. Allison, Philip B. Heymann, Mancur Olson, Howard Raiffa, Charles L. Schultze, Edith M. Stokey, A. Michael Spence, and Richard J. Zeckhauser.

If the book reads well it is largely because Joyce Huntley Quelch types superb copy with such speed and good humor, while doing everything else that a secretary does, that I enjoyed the luxury of unlimited revisions.

Parts of Chapters 3 and 4 were in Robin Marris (ed.), *The Corporate Society* (Macmillan, 1974) and are used here by permission of the President and Fellows of Harvard University. An earlier version of Chapter 5 was in Bela Balassa and Richard Nelson (eds.), *Economic Progress, Private Values, and Public Policy* (North-Holland Publishing Company, 1977). A longer version of Chapter 7 appeared as

7

"Hockey Helmets, Concealed Weapons, and Daylight Saving: A Study of Binary Choices with Externalities," *Journal of Conflict Resolution*, Vol. 17, No. 3 (September 1973), pp. 381–428 and is used here by permission of the publisher, Sage Publications, Inc.

1

MICROMOTIVES AND
MACROBEHAVIOR

I WAS INVITED once to give a lecture to a large audience; the program was to begin at 8:00 in the evening. I followed my escort into the building through the stage entrance and stood in the wings as a microphone was put around my neck. I could see the first dozen rows: nobody had arrived. I assumed that 8:00 meant 8:15, as it might at an academic gathering, and was puzzled when my host walked on stage, nodded to the rows of empty seats, and went through the motions of introducing me. Resisting slightly, I was pushed gently out of the wings and toward the rostrum.

There were eight hundred people in the hall, densely packed from the thirteenth row to the distant rear wall. Feeling a little as though I were addressing a crowd on the opposite bank of a river, I gave my lecture. Afterwards, I asked my hosts why they had arranged the seating that way.

They hadn't.

There were no seating arrangements and no ushers. The arrangement was voluntary, and could only reflect the preferences of the audience. What are we to suppose those preferences were?

It is possible that everybody preferred the whole audience to pack itself into the two dozen rows toward the rear, leaving the first dozen vacant. But, except for any example he set, nobody controlled where anybody else sat. People did not vote with their bottoms on a seating plan. All they did was to choose where to sit from among the available seats they could see as they scanned the hall while walking down the aisle.

Can we guess what policy people followed in choosing their seats? I should add that, as far as I could tell, nothing differentiated the people in different rows. People toward the front or rear did not seem to be older or better dressed or predominately male or female. Those in the front—the thirteenth row—may have seemed more attentive than the rest but they probably knew that, even at that distance, I could see their eyelids droop or their heads nod, and were motivated to stay a little more alert.

Curious as I was, I neglected to ask my hosts about the order in which the different rows were filled. Did they fill in sequence from back to front? Did people distribute themselves at random among the rearward two dozen rows? Or did the first arrivals fill the thirteenth row, later arrivals filling the rows in sequence toward the rear? That last is improbable: it would be a coincidence if the earliest arrivals had chosen a forward boundary that would ultimately hold, densely packed, exactly the number of people who showed up. The dynamics had to be consistent with the populating of a compact area by people who could not know how many would be arriving later.

There are several reasons we might interest ourselves in what it is that those people were doing, or thought they were doing, or were trying to do, when they seated themselves in that way. One is that we do not like the result; we prefer they all be in the first twenty-four rows, not the last twenty-four, or distributed over the whole auditorium. If we want to change the pattern with a minimum of organization, interfering as little as possible with the preferences of the audience, we need to know whether we can subtly change their incentives or their perceptions of the auditorium so that they will "voluntarily" choose a better seating pattern.

And before we do any such thing we ought to know whether the audience itself likes the seating arrangement that it chose, and whether the fact that they chose their seats as they did is evidence that they must be satisfied with the outcome.

A second reason for interest is that there may be something about this process that reminds us of other situations in which people locate themselves voluntarily in some pattern that does not possess evident advantages even for the people who by their own choices form the pattern. Residential location is an example. This laboratory experiment in the auditorium can give us hints of what to look for in other situations.

My immediate purpose in inviting you to speculate on the motives that led to that seating pattern is neither to develop a handbook of auditorium management nor to draw analogies with residential choice or the behavior of crowds or the filling of parking lots. It is to give a vivid example of what this book is about. What this book is about is a kind of analysis that is characteristic of a large part of the social sciences, especially the more theoretical part. That kind of analysis explores the relation between the behavior characteristics of the *individuals* who comprise some social aggregate, and the characteristics of the *aggregate*.

This analysis sometimes uses what is known about individual intentions to predict the aggregates: if we know that people entering an auditorium have a sociable desire to sit near somebody but always to leave one empty seat between them, we can predict something about the pattern that will appear when the entire audience has arrived. Alternatively this kind of analysis may do what I invited you to do—to try to figure out what intentions, or modes of behavior, of separate individuals could lead to the pattern we observed. If there are several plausible behaviors that could lead to what we observed, we can look for evidence by which to choose among them.

There are easy cases, of course, in which the aggregate is merely an extrapolation from the individual. If we know that every driver, on his own, turns his lights on at sundown, we can guess that from our helicopter we shall see all the car lights in a local area going on at about the same time. We could even get our compass bearings by reflecting that the cascade of lights on the Massachusetts Turnpike will flow westward as dusk settles. But if most people turn their lights on when some fraction of the oncoming cars already have their lights on, we'll get a different picture from our helicopter. In the second case, drivers are responding to each other's behav-

ior and influencing each other's behavior. People are responding to an environment that consists of other people responding
to *their* environment, which consists of people responding to
an environment of people's responses. Sometimes the dynamics
are sequential: if your lights induce me to turn mine on, mine
may induce somebody else but not you. Sometimes the
dynamics are reciprocal: hearing your car horn, I honk mine,
thus encouraging you to honk more insistently.

These situations, in which people's behavior or people's
choices depend on the behavior or the choices of other people,
are the ones that usually don't permit any simple summation or
extrapolation to the aggregates. To make that connection we
usually have to look at the *system of interaction* between individuals and their environment, that is, between individuals
and other individuals or between individuals and the collectiv-
ity. And sometimes the results are surprising. Sometimes they
are not easily guessed. Sometimes the analysis is difficult.
Sometimes it is inconclusive. But even inconclusive analysis
can warn against jumping to conclusions about individual
intentions from observations of aggregates, or jumping to conclusions about the behavior of aggregates from what one
knows or can guess about individual intentions.

Return to that audience of mine and speculate a little on
the motives that might lead people to sit as they did. (We
needn't assume that they all had the same intentions.) What
are some plausible conjectures—alternative hypotheses—about
what it is that those people were doing that could lead to the
result I described? How do we evaluate the result in the light
of each hypothesis? How might we influence the result,
according to different hypotheses? How much leeway does
each hypothesis allow for the role of chance, or architecture?
And can we investigate the several hypotheses, to choose
among them, or to reject them all and keep looking?

An obvious possibility is that everybody likes to sit as
close to the rear as possible. The earliest arrivals get to sit farthest to the rear; late arrivals can wish they had come earlier,

but there's no way to improve on the outcome for the whole audience by switching people around because for everybody we might switch to the rear there would be somebody who had to go forward. Blocking off the last dozen rows would translate them all a dozen seats forward, if that's where we want them.

A second possibility, not the same thing, is that everybody wants to sit to the rear of everybody else—not to the rear of the hall, just behind the other people. (Maybe they like to get out first afterward.) They may prefer everybody else to be as far forward as possible, so they, too, can be as far forward as possible, still staying behind everybody. To do that the early arrivals sit far enough back to make allowance for later arrivals, who then sit behind them, not forward; or, if the early arrivals attribute the same behavior to those who will come later, they have to choose the row farthest to the rear or people will crowd in behind them. Again, blocking off the last dozen rows will translate them all forward, if that's where we want them, and maybe that's where they'd like to be. They just didn't get there.

A third possibility is that everybody wants to sit where he is close to people, either to be sociable or to avoid being conspicuously alone. If the first few arrivals happen to sit toward the rear, later arrivals will congregate there until the populated area has reached the back. From then on there's no room except toward the front, and to be near people the last arrivals fill the rows immediately forward of those who are already there. If we could get the first few people to sit toward the front, the same process would lead to the reverse result: late arrivals, finding the front full, would fill the rows immediately behind. Either way the early arrivals get surrounded and everybody is bunched. But in one case they are sitting down front and in the other toward the rear. We may like one result better. Or they may like it better.

A fourth possibility is that everybody likes to watch the audience come in, as people do at weddings. To avoid craning their necks and being seen staring, they sit as far to the rear as possible and watch as people walk by and down the aisle. Once the audience is seated there is no advantage in sitting to the rear—either to the rear of the other people, or to the rear of the auditorium. If we could estimate the size of the crowd and block off the back rows, everybody could indulge his sightseeing and be twelve rows closer to what's going on, and there wouldn't be that embarrassing moat between the speaker and the audience. Or if we had people enter from the front instead of the rear, the early arrivals could combine better seats in front with the same opportunity to watch later arrivals come in.

Still another hypothesis is that most members of the audience developed their seating habits in other times and places, where they found disadvantages in sitting down front. Without thinking about it, they sat toward the rear as they always do, later realizing perhaps that there was no teacher to call on students in the front row and that they could just as well have sat forward and seen and heard better. And so forth. We could even propose that people are merely tired and take the nearest vacant seat when they enter the room. But that behavior would have to be coupled with a rule of decorum—that the first person in any row must go midway between the two aisles and the next people must move alongside to minimize the climbing over—for this "minimum effort" hypothesis to give us the result we observed.

There is one hypothesis that I find interesting because it is so minimal, yet sufficient. This is that nobody cares where he sits, as long as it's not in the very front—not in the first occupied row. Out of two dozen rows that might be partially filled, a person is indifferent among 23 of them. He just does not want to sit in the first one.

Actually, everybody may want to sit as far *forward* as possible, subject to the single proviso that he not be in the first occupied row. To be on the safe side, and not knowing how large the audience will be, people sit toward the rear; as it begins to look as though most of the audience has arrived, people will climb over seated people to occupy empty seats in the crowded section rather than enter that vacant row just in front of everybody else.

Somebody, of course, ends up sitting in front of everybody. And they might all be just as happy, or happier, if the entire audience were shifted 12 rows forward. The people in the other 23 rows surely would prefer to have the whole crowd shifted forward.

An even weaker hypothesis is that people don't even mind being in the very first occupied row as long as the rows immediately behind them are filled, so they are not conspicuously down front by themselves. That can lead to the same result.

Purposive Behavior

Notice that in all of these hypotheses there is a notion of people's having preferences, pursuing goals, minimizing effort or embarrassment or maximizing view or comfort, seeking company or avoiding it, and otherwise behaving in a way that we might call "purposive." Furthermore, the goals or purposes or objectives relate directly to other people and *their* behavior, or are constrained by an environment that consists of other people who are pursuing their goals or their purposes or their objectives. What we typically have is a mode of *contingent behavior*—behavior that depends on what others are doing.

In other sciences, and sometimes in the social sciences, we metaphorically ascribe motives to behavior because something behaves *as if* it were oriented toward a goal. Water seeks its own level. Nature abhors a vacuum. Soap bubbles minimize surface tension and light travels a path that, allowing for different speeds through different media, minimizes travel time. But if we fill a J-shaped tube with water and close the lower end so that the water in the pipe cannot achieve its own level, nobody really supposes that the water feels frustrated. And if we then open the lower end of the tube so that most of the water spills on the floor, nobody imputes shortsightedness to the water for having only spilt itself in seeking its own level. Most of us don't think that light is really in a hurry. Lately there are some amongst us who think that sunflowers are anguished if they cannot follow the sun, and we are told that leaves seek positions on trees that divide the sunlight among them to maximize photosynthesis. If we are in the lumber business we like the leaves to succeed, but not for their sake; we might not even be sure whether the leaves are acting on their own or are merely slaves to an enzyme, or parts of a chemical system for which words like "purpose" and "seek" are wholly nonascriptive and nonevaluative.

But with people it's different. When we analyze how people behave in trying to escape from a burning building we mean that they really are trying to escape. They are not simply acting "as if" they dislike being burnt. With people, in contrast to light beams and water, we usually believe we are dealing with conscious decisions or adaptations in the pursuit of goals, immediate or remote, within the limits of their information and their comprehension of how to navigate through their environment toward whatever their objectives are. In fact, we can often ascribe to people some capacity to solve problems—to calculate or to perceive intuitively how to get from here to there. And if we know what problem a person is trying to solve, and if we think he actually can solve it, and if we can solve it too, we can anticipate what our subject will do by putting ourself in his place and solving his problem as we think he sees it. This is the method of "vicarious problem solving" that underlies most of microeconomics.

An advantage in dealing with "goal-seeking" unconscious substances, like the water that seeks its own level or, in biology, the genes that seek to protect and proliferate genes like themselves, is that we are not likely to forget that the motives we ascribe are no more than a convenience of expression, a suggestive analogy or a useful formula. With people, we can get carried away with our image of goal seeking and problem solving. We can forget that people pursue misguided goals or don't know their goals, and that they enjoy or suffer subconscious processes that deceive them about their goals. And we can exaggerate how much good is accomplished when people achieve the goals we think they think they have been pursuing.

Nevertheless, this style of analysis undeniably invites evaluation. It is hard to explore what happens when people behave with a purpose without becoming curious, even concerned, about how well or how badly the outcome serves the purpose. Social scientists are more like forest rangers than like naturalists. The naturalist can be interested in what causes a species to become extinct, without caring whether or not it does become extinct. (If it has been extinct for a million years his curiosity is surely without concern.) The ranger will be concerned with whether or not the buffalo do disappear, and how to keep them in a healthy balance with their environment.

What makes this evaluation interesting and difficult is that the entire aggregate outcome is what has to be evaluated, not merely how each person does within the constraints of his own environment. In a burning building it may be wise to run, not walk, to the nearest exit, especially if everybody else is running; what has to be evaluated is how many get safely out of the building if, each doing the best he can to save himself, they all run. Everyone who entered my auditorium may have done a good job of picking the best seat available at the moment he entered the room. (Some may have wished, after all eight hundred had taken their seats, that they *had* sat a little farther front when they saw where everybody else sat and how many others arrived.) But the most interesting question is not how many people would like to change their seats after they see where everybody else is sitting; it is whether some altogether different seating arrangement might better serve the purposes of many, or most, or all of them.

How well each does for himself in adapting to his social environment is not the same thing as how satisfactory a social environment they collectively create for themselves.

Market Behavior

Among the social sciences the one that conforms most to the kind of analysis I have been describing is economics. In economics the "individuals" are people, families, owners of farms and businesses, taxi drivers, managers of banks and insurance companies, doctors and school teachers and soldiers, and people who work for the banks and the mining companies. Most people, whether they drive their own taxis or manage continent-wide airlines, are expected to know very little about the whole economy and the way it works. They know the prices of the things they buy and sell, the interest rates at which they lend and borrow, and something about the pertinent alternatives to the ways they are currently earning their living or running their business or spending their money. The dairy farmer doesn't need to know how many people eat butter and how far away they are, how many other people raise cows, how many babies drink milk, or whether more money is spent on beer than on milk. What he needs to know is the prices of different feeds, the characteristics of different cows, the different prices farmers are getting for milk according to its butter fat content, the relative costs of hired labor and electrical machinery, and what his net earnings might be if he sold his cows and raised pigs instead or sold his farm and took the best job for which he's qualified in some city he is willing to live in.

Somehow all of the activities seem to get coordinated. There's a taxi to get you to the airport. There's butter and cheese for lunch on the airplane. There are refineries to make the airplane fuel and trucks to transport it, cement for the runways, electricity for the escalators, and, most important of all, passengers who want to fly where the airplanes are going.

The fact that there is never a taxi when you need one in the rain, or that you can fly 3,000 miles more comfortably than you can fly 300 and flights are occasionally overbooked, reminds us how spoiled we are. We expect this fantastically complex system to be even better coordinated than it sometimes is. Tens of millions of people making billions of decisions every week about what to buy and what to sell and where to work and how much to save and how much to borrow and what orders to fill and what stocks to accumulate and where to move and what schools to go to and what jobs to take and where to build the supermarkets and movie theatres and electric power stations, when to invest in buildings above ground and mine shafts underground and fleets of trucks and ships and aircraft—if you are in a mood to be amazed, it can amaze you that the system works at all. Amazement needn't be admiration: once you understand the system you may think there are better ones, or better ways to make this system work. I am only inviting you to reflect that whether this system works well or ill, in most countries and especially the countries with comparatively undirected economic systems, the system works the way ant colonies work.

It is generally not believed that any ant in an ant colony knows how the ant colony works. Each ant has certain things that it does, in coordinated association with other ants, but there is nobody minding the whole store. No ant designed the system. An important part of social biology is relating the world of the individual ant to the world of the ant colony. The colony is full of patterns and regularities and balanced proportions among different activities, with maintenance and repair and exploration and even mobilization for emergencies. But no individual ant knows whether there are too few or too many ants exploring for food or rebuilding after a thunderstorm or helping to carry in the carcass of a beetle. Each ant lives in its own little world, responding to the other ants in its immediate environment and responding to signals of which it does not know the origin. Why the system works as it does, and as effectively as it does, is a dynamic problem of social and genetic evolution. How it works—how it is that the limited set of choices made by each ant within its own truncated little world translates, in the aggregate, into the rich and seemingly

meaningful pattern of aggregate behavior by which we
describe the society and the economy of the ant—is a question
akin to the question of how it is that all the cows know how
much milk is needed to make the butter and the cheese and
the ice cream that people will buy at a price that covers the
cost of maintaining and milking the cow and getting each little
piece of butter wrapped in aluminum foil with the airline's
own insignia printed on it.

What I asked you to be amazed at, and not necessarily to
admire, is simply the enormous complexity of the entire collective system of behavior, a system that the individuals who
comprise the system needn't know anything about or even be
aware of. If we see pattern and order and regularity, we
should withhold judgment about whether it is the pattern and
order of a jungle, a slave system, or a community infested by
parasitic diseases, and inquire first of all what it is that the
individuals who comprise the system seem to be doing and
how it is that their actions, in the large, produce the patterns
we see. Then we can try to evaluate whether, at least according to what the individuals are trying to do, the resulting pattern is in some way responsive to their intentions.

In economics it often appears that a lot of this unmanaged
and unguided individual activity leads to aggregate results
that are not too bad, indeed about as good as could be
expected if somebody took command and figured out what
ought to be done and had a way to get everybody to do what
he was supposed to do. Two hundred years ago Adam Smith
characterized the system as one that worked *as if* some unseen
hand brought about the coordination.

Actually, economists do not usually make careful observations, compare what they observe with alternatives they can
imagine, and judge the results to be good. What they do is to
infer, from what they take to be the behavior characteristics of
people, some of the characteristics of the system as a whole,
and *deduce* some evaluative conclusions. If Canadian farmers
ship too many Christmas trees to Albany and not enough to

Buffalo, sellers in Buffalo will be able to sell their trees for more than trees are going for in Albany and somebody will buy trees in Albany and send them overnight by truck to Buffalo and the next day there will be a more "balanced" distribution of trees between the two cities, the balance reflecting how badly people in the two cities want Christmas trees compared with the other things that their money will buy. And so forth.

The result is often characterized by the statement that "the market works." By "market" is meant the entire complex of institutions within which people buy and sell and hire and are hired and borrow and lend and trade and contract and shop around to find bargains. A lot may be wrong with the deductive reasoning of economists, but when they state the conclusion carefully and modestly they have a point. The free market may not do much, or anything, to distribute opportunities and resources among people the way you or I might like them distributed, and it may not lead people to like the activities we wish they liked or to want to consume the things we wish they wanted to consume; it may encourage individualist rather than group values and it may fail to protect people against their own shortsightedness and self-indulgence. It may lead to asymmetrical personal relationships between employee and employer, lender and borrower, and attach too much status to material attainments. The market may even perform disastrously where inflation and depression are concerned. Still, within those serious limitations, it does remarkably well in coordinating or harmonizing or integrating the efforts of myriads of self-serving individuals and organizations.

For my purpose there's no need to reach a judgment about just how well the "free market" does what is attributed to it, or whether it does it at a price worth paying. I am interested here in how much promise the economist's result has outside economics. If economists have studied the matter for two hundred years and many of them have concluded that a comparatively unrestricted free market is often an advantageous way of letting individuals interact with each other, should we suppose that the same is true in all the rest of those social activities, the ones that do not fall under the heading of economics, in which people impinge upon people as they go about pursuing their own interests? Presently I shall enumerate and discuss some of those other activities (aside from choosing seats in an auditorium), but as illustration let me mention the languages we speak and how we speak them, whom we marry and whether we have children and what names we give our children, whom we live near and whom we choose for friends, what games we play and what customs we develop, what fashions we pursue, whether we walk the streets or stay indoors, how we drive cars or make noise or smoke in public, the pets we keep and how we manage them. Then there are eating and drinking habits, and the times of day for going to lunch; littering and habits of cleanliness and sanitation; the transmission of jokes and gossip and news and useful information; the formation of parties and movements; and whether we wait in line for our turn.

All of these are activities in which people's behavior is influenced by the behavior of others, or people care about the behavior of others, or they both care and are influenced. Most of these activities are substantially free of centralized management in many societies, including our own, or subject to sanctions and proscriptions that work indirectly. (The dictionary may eventually tell me what a seven-year-old means by "dynamite," but that's not where the seven-year-old learned to say it.) And though people may care how it all comes out in the aggregate, their *own* decisions and their *own* behavior are typically motivated toward their *own* interests, and often impinged on by only a local fragment of the overall pattern. Hardly anybody who marries a tall person, or a short person, is much motivated by what it will do to the frequency distribution of body height in the next generation. But the next generation's notions of what is tall and what is short will be affected by whether in this generation tall people marry tall people and short people short, or tall and short marry each other, or everybody marries at random.

Equilibrium Analysis

In a moment I am going to argue that there is no presumption that the self-serving behavior of individuals should usually lead to collectively satisfactory results. Economics covers a special case—a large and important special case, but a special case—and I am going to identify what makes economics a special case.

But before that I need to dispose of a false issue that gets too much attention. A method of analysis that is common in economics, common in biology, and common also in many of the non–life-related sciences, is the study of "equilibria." An equilibrium is a situation in which some motion or activity or adjustment or response has died away, leaving something stationary, at rest, "in balance," or in which several things that have been interacting, adjusting to each other and to each other's adjustment, are at last adjusted, in balance, at rest. If you pour cream in your coffee there will be one kind of "equilibrium" when the surface has stopped rippling, and another when the cream is either dispersed evenly through the coffee or floating as a film on the surface. In economics there is an "equilibrium" distribution of Christmas trees, relative to the demand for Christmas trees, if prices are similar enough from city to city, or city to suburb, so that nobody can make money by moving trees from downtown to the suburbs or from Albany to Buffalo. There is equilibrium in the market for gasoline if prices from place to place do not differ more than transport costs between those places, and if the average price is one at which the amount of gasoline that people are willing to buy is in balance with the amount that producers can profitably put on the market. And so forth.

An equilibrium can be exact or approximate. It can be always approached but never quite achieved, the potential equilibrium itself continually changing. And equilibrium can be partial or more complete, short run or long run. Christmas trees can be in balance among the cities, but an overall over-supply means that shippers of Christmas trees will lose money this year and next year fewer trees will be provided and the market may or may not be in equilibrium by next year or the year after.

The point to make here is that there is nothing particularly attractive about an equilibrium. An equilibrium is simply a result. It is what is there after something has settled down, if something ever does settle down. The idea of equilibrium is an acknowledgment that there are adjustment processes; and unless one is particularly interested in *how* dust settles, one can simplify analysis by concentrating on what happens after the dust has settled. In Malthusian analysis, the population is "in equilibrium" when the supply of food and other natural resources is so meager, relative to the population, that a low birthrate and a high death rate keep the population stationary. A public beach in the summertime is in equilibrium when it is so crowded that it is no longer attractive to anyone who might have wanted to go to the beach, but not quite so unattractive that the people who are already there give up and go home. The world's whale population is in equilibrium when the remaining whales are so few that hardly anybody can catch enough to make a good business out of it, and the few whalers who have nothing better to do are just able to catch enough whales to offset the new births in the small population. High-way speeds are in equilibrium vis-a-vis the state police when arrests are just frequent enough to offset the urge to drive a little faster. And so forth.

There may be many things wrong with "equilibrium analysis," including the possibility that it oversimplifies by neglecting processes of adjustment, or exaggerates the prevalence of equilibrium by neglecting shifts in the parameters that determine the equilibrium. But nobody should resist "equilibrium analysis" for fear that, if he acknowledges that something is in equilibrium, he will have acknowledged that something is all right. The body of a hanged man is in equilibrium when it finally stops swinging, but nobody is going to insist that the man is all right. An unnecessary source of distrust of economic analysis is the assumption that when an economist discusses equilibrium he is expressing approval. I believe that assumption is usually—not always, but usually—a mistake.

The difference between economics and those other social phenomena will not, therefore, be a difference in the mode of analysis, and especially will not be that the one deals with equilibrium systems, rightly or wrongly, and the others do not. An economist would describe the seating pattern in our auditorium in terms of equilibria just as he would the market for air conditioning. The seating pattern is an equilibrium if, considering where everybody else is sitting, nobody is motivated to move to another seat. Calling it an equilibrium does not imply that everybody—or even anybody likes the seating arrangement, only that nobody alone can do better by changing to any available seat. Nor does it imply that there are not alternative seating patterns, very different ones, that could also be equilibria.

Exchanges and Other Transactions

To identify what makes economics a large and important special case, rather than a model for all social phenomena, let me remind you of the particular characteristics of all of these behavior systems that I am trying to focus on. It is that people are impinging on other people and adapting to other people. What people do affects what other people do. How well people accomplish what they want to accomplish depends on what others are doing. How you drive depends on how others drive; where you park depends on where others park. Your vocabulary and your pronunciation depend on the vocabularies and accents of others. Whom you marry depends on whom you meet, who will marry you, and who is already married. If your problem is that there is too much traffic, you are part of the problem. If you join a crowd because you like crowds, you add to the crowd. If you withdraw your child from school because of the pupils he goes to school with, you remove a pupil that *they* go to school with. If you raise your voice to make yourself heard, you add to the noise that other people are raising their voices to be heard above. When you cut your hair short you change, ever so slightly, other people's impressions of how long people are wearing their hair.

Sometimes you care what it is that the others are doing: you wish fewer were driving when the traffic gets thick. Sometimes you don't care but you need to adapt: it doesn't matter whether you have the right-of-way going uphill or downhill, as long as you know who has the right-of-way. Usually you both care and are influenced. (If you neither care nor are influenced, then it's outside what this book is about.)

Now for what is special about economics. Economics is mainly concerned with transactions in which *everybody affected is a voluntary participant*. The epitome is trading vegetables for eggs over the back fence. On certain conditions, this is a "good thing." You wouldn't do it unless you wanted the eggs more than the vegetables and your neighbor wouldn't unless he wanted the vegetables more than the eggs. Nobody else cares or needs to know whether you have a hard boiled egg or a lettuce-and-tomato sandwich for lunch.

Of course this is an exaggeration:

Eggs may have more cholesterol than is good for you.
Your neighbor may steal eggs because he knows that you'll trade vegetables for them.
Somebody may believe that chicken farms are cruel.
The neighbor who traded with you may have known that the egg was diseased.
And, when he cooks the cabbage you traded him, the family upstairs may be offended by the smell.

Still, the traditional subject of economics has been voluntary exchanges, exchanges that do not have major implications for all the people who do not participate in the transaction and who have no opportunity to veto it. If anybody affected is part of the transaction; if the transaction is voluntary and anybody who legitimately objects can veto it; if the transaction is easy to recognize and people know their own interests, so that interested parties can protect their interests by participating or blocking the transaction; if people do not make themselves vulnerable to theft and extortion and the like when they manifest an interest in the transaction; if the people who bring their vegetables to market will be protected against theft; and, if the law will prevent people from improperly creating demand for their products by poisoning other people's chickens, then there is a lot to be said for treating "free-market exchange" as a good thing. At least it is a good thing if we think it a good thing for people to have more of what they like when they can have it at nobody else's expense.

There are a lot of requirements for making the free market work well, or even work at all. In addition to physical protection and contract enforcement, there has to be a lot of shopping around so that people know what trades are available, or enough information so that without shopping around people know what to expect when they buy or sell. Behind a typical free market is centuries of patient development of property rights and other legal arrangements, and an extraordinary standardization of goods and services and the terminology for describing them. Think of all the things you can actually purchase by telephone, confident that you will get what you asked for or be able to tell the difference at a glance. A lot of legal and institutional arrangements are designed to protect the rights of people who might, though affected by a transaction, be left out of it.

Economists are aware of a multitude of reasons why markets may not work to everybody's satisfaction. I have mentioned some. People lack the knowledge to shop around for medical care. It is hard to tell a good secondhand auto from a bad one, or a fraudulent repair job from an honest one. It is hard to sell a secret without giving it away. Some markets are easily monopolized, and economists don't expect monopolized markets to work well. In identifying these problem cases, economists customarily ask why it is that the market doesn't work, and they have a pretty good checklist to help them in their diagnoses. The market for brave watchmen will fail if the obligation to be brave in an emergency is unenforceable; for life insurance if the insurance company cannot tell who the high-risk customers are but the high-risk customers know; for cancer medicine if people are misinformed or superstitious about what will cure their affliction, or easily mistaken about whether they have the disease; for dangerous machinery if people are ignorant of the dangers; for broadcast news and weather reports if everybody can listen free of charge; for public swimming pools if users cannot be monitored against fouling the pool; for betting on sports events if heavy bettors can interfere in the health and safety of the players; for telephone service if some part of the enterprise has to be consolidated into a single interconnected network, hence a monopoly; for right-of-way at an intersection because the drivers of competing cars and trucks have no way to communicate offers and agreements.

Notice that in all these cases there was some initial reason to expect that the market might work. Upon inspection it turns out that although the market indeed can work for certain kinds of medicine and certain kinds of information and certain kinds of insurance and certain kinds of performance contracts, it might not work, or not work well, for these particular kinds, for reasons that can be analytically diagnosed.

There are also the markets we don't like that work entirely too well; for example, the market for stolen goods, which encourages burglary, the markets for votes and fixed traffic tickets and political favors and falsified inspection certificates, even a market for kidnapped businessmen—things that are not supposed to be for sale.

I'll complain if nobody buys my book, especially if somebody writes a better one and gets all the business, but I probably shouldn't blame that on "the market." When I mentioned that economics is mainly concerned with market transactions in which everybody affected is a voluntary participant I should have mentioned a qualification: if you buy somebody else's book, I may feel "affected" by the transaction because the alternative I had in mind was selling you my book instead. I can wish that people wanted, and would pay for, the things I have to offer, and would offer me, at attractive prices, the things I would like to buy; but this is more like wishing for transactions that didn't occur than objecting to some that did.

What the market is often so good at doing is only part of what happens in the market. While coordinating activities efficiently, the market may produce a distribution of income that you and I do not like, either in general, or just because of where it leaves us. This is why I invited only your amazement, not your admiration, of what the market can perform (or, even if your admiration, not necessarily your unqualified approval).

But now look at an activity that at first glance is like a "market activity" but upon closer inspection isn't. To make my point I'll choose a non-controversial illustration familiar to most of us, the "non-market" for Christmas cards. There is a literal market for Christmas cards—a market for buying them, and a federally monopolized market for sending them by mail. But I mean the choosing of whom to send a card to, what kind of card, how expensive, by what date to mail it, whether to pen a message, and what to do about non-Christian addressees. In addition to personal greetings we have cards from teachers to students and students to teachers, elected officials to their constituents and insurance salesmen to their policyholders, and, of course, from your paperboy or papergirl.

My impression—and I've found nobody who doesn't share it—is that the sending of Christmas cards is an "interactive process" greatly affected by custom and by expectations of what others expect and what others may send, by cards received (and not received) last year and already received this year, conditioned of course by the cost of cards and postage and the labor as well as the fun or nuisance of selecting cards and penning inscriptions.

People feel obliged to send cards to people from whom

they expect to receive them, often knowing that they will receive them only because the senders expect to receive cards in return. People sometimes send cards only because, cards having been sent for several years, cessation might signal something. People send cards early to avoid the suspicion that they were sent only after one had already been received. Students send cards to teachers believing that other students do. Sensible people who might readily agree to stop bothering each other with Christmas cards find it embarrassing, or not quite worth the trouble, to reach such agreement. (If they could, they might be so pleased that they would celebrate by sending "voluntary" cards, falling back into the trap!)

My casual inquiry suggests widespread if not unanimous opinion that the system has some of the characteristics of a trap. Even people who, on balance, like Christmas cards find parts of the system ludicrous, preposterous, or downright infuriating. Some wish the whole institution could be wiped out. Some wish for a "bankruptcy" proceeding in which all Christmas-card lists could be obliterated so people could start over, motivated only by friendship and holiday spirit, without accumulated obligations.

Nobody claims that the system reaches optimal results. Even if everybody guesses correctly the cards he will receive, and ends the holiday season with no regrets for the cards he sent and the cards he didn't send, the outcome is a long way from ideal. And there isn't much that anybody can do about it.

Fortunately, it doesn't matter much.

At first glance someone might call this exchange of greetings a "free market activity." But "exchange" is an ironic metaphor. And "market" is a remote and unhelpful analogy. Things don't work out optimally for a simple reason: there is no reason why they should. There is no mechanism that attunes individual responses to some collective accomplishment.

It cannot even be argued that if the whole system worked badly enough it would become extinct. There is no mechanism that would induce people to stop sending cards merely because everybody, like everybody else, deplored the system and wished it would disappear.

There was a time when wise people thought planets should revolve in circles. When observation showed incontrovertibly that they did not, the question was asked, "Why not?" People tried to figure what kept the planets from displaying perfect circles. In the end it was realized that, in accordance with the laws of motion and gravitation, there never had been any reasons to expect circles. Circles were not the norm; ellipses were.

When we ask why the "free market" in Christmas cards doesn't lead to optimal exchange, the answer is that it is not a market and there was no reason to expect optimal results in the first place. The free market, when it works, is that special case of knowledgeable voluntary exchange of alienable commodities. Only some ellipses are circles.

Contrived Markets and Partial Markets

I must add two qualifications, one that enlarges the scope for market arrangements and one that reduces it. The first is that it is often possible, by legal and institutional innovation, to endow activities with the characteristics that make markets. The legal invention of "copyright" makes the written word a marketable commodity. Just as a woodcutter wouldn't cut wood if bystanders were free to carry it away as fast as he cut it, writers might not write if people could freely copy everything they so painfully and skillfully compose. Property law doesn't let me pick your vegetables and give them to my friends; by extending the concept of "property" to original compositions, the law does not permit *me* to sell a copy of what *you* have written until you sell me the right to do it.

The beach that is so overcrowded on a hot day that many people are not attracted and some leave in disgust (and even those that remain don't enjoy it much) can be better exploited by the people to whom the beach belongs if attendance is regulated by an admission fee, the proceeds accruing to the people whose beach it is. Or admissions can be rationed among beachgoers, in numbers calculated to enhance the collective enjoyment of the beach, with people who adore bathing free to buy admissions from people who would rather have more money than swim.

These are not "free-market arrangements." They require the intervention of some authority to set up a system of management. But the system is modelled on market principles. Creating something like a market is a principle of wide usefulness. But is far from universally applicable. It works with the crowds at public beaches but not with the crowds that gather to watch a building burn, obstructing the firefighters and causing the building to burn more brightly. Copyright laws will not keep people from passing malicious rumors, or spoiling a suspense movie by telling its ending.

The second qualification is that markets often appear to work toward greater harmony than they do. Some social consequences have been left out of account. A market appears to do a pretty good job of allocating houses and apartments to people who need places to live. But it matches people only with living quarters, not with neighbors; the demographic, ethnic, and cultural patterns of living will be determined in the entire interactive process of choosing homes and neighbors and neighborhoods. The market transactions involve only the landlord and tenant.

The market may appear to work well for the production and distribution of perfumes, deodorants, and portable radios, but there is no market which determines their use or non-use by locally interested parties.

The market for pets does not reflect the interest of bird lovers in the market for cats, or of cat lovers in the market for dogs, or the interest of people who walk sidewalks in the market for animals that foul the footpath. Indeed, the interactive phenomenon of pet ownership, and the training and management and mismanagement of pets, is an extensive social activity of which only a modest part shows up in the market for animals, animal food, veterinary services, and, occasionally, poison.

Of all the activities that fall within my subject one of the most important is on the borderline of "market arrangements." That is marriage. Aside from everything else that it is, marriage in this country is a voluntary contractual arrangement between people who are free to shop around. The parties most affected are the two who make the contract. Each offers something complementary to the other, and there is expected an economical division of labor. The relationship is asymmetrical in many ways; but so are the contractual relations between people and their nursemaids, housekeepers, business partners, mountaineering guides, tutors, pilots, and income-tax accountants. There is more here than just a remote analogy with long-term bilateral exclusive-service contracts. The legal status is somewhat contractual and becoming more so; and one can imagine secular societies in which marriage would be assimilated to contract law. To refuse on sentimental or religious grounds to acknowledge this is to miss an important characteristic of getting married.

But to treat it as just another private long-term reciprocal exclusive-service contract would be to miss even more important characteristics of marriage. Except for the very rich, the very famous, and sometimes the ethnically loyal, marriage is very privately motivated. The marriage choice is constrained by language, religion, geography, and education, but people get married because they want to and the selection of a mate is not part of a genetic or cultural plan. Yet marital choices in the aggregate have enormous influence on the genetic, religious, linguistic, socio-economic, and geographical makeup of the next generation. Marriage itself, children aside, affects language and religion and social mobility and the dispersion or concentration of tastes and habits and customs. Even the unmarried are greatly influenced by the frequency of marriage in their age group. Racial and religious separatism are drastically affected by the racial and religious makeup of married couples. Economic and occupational mobility are affected by the matching or non-matching in marriage of income levels and occupational backgrounds, skills and talents and intelligence, disabilities and handicaps.

The social consequences of marriage make this activity one of the central phenomena in the landscape of social science. The fact that it is in important respects a market process only informs us about one of its dimensions.

Interactive Behaviors

It is time to give a more extensive enumeration of social activities of the kind I have been discussing. To begin, go back to the audience in the auditorium and branch out from there. That audience was an example of *spatial distribution*. Besides auditoriums it occurs in the way people distribute themselves on beaches or toward the front of a bus, in the way people who push out of a crowded theatre stand idly on the sidewalk afterwards blocking the egress of the people still pushing out of the theatre, the way people congregate at standup parties and receptions, and the way people form crowds at a rally, a riot, or a spectacle. On a larger scale it shows up in residential patterns. In motion it occurs in racing for the exit in a baseball park or evacuating the parking lot after the ballgame, in the spacing of cars on a highway, and in the arrival times of people who form queues to board a plane or to take seats at a performance.

There is no single mode of behavior that covers all these cases. Sometimes people want to be close, sometimes spread out; the people on the edge of a crowd may be pushing to get in and the people in the middle are being crushed. If everybody likes to be in the middle of a crowd, the crowd will be dense; if everybody prefers to be on the edge of a crowd, the crowd will be dispersed, and may even fail to be a crowd.

More complex is the behavior of people who want to be close to or distant from particular kinds of other people.

People get separated and integrated by sex, race, age, language, dress or social status, or by patterns of acquaintance and friendship. The motives of individuals can lead to striking and unexpected collective results.

At many colleges that have recently become co-educational, or have recently given up segregating the sexes, the question arises, how might the men and the women distribute themselves among the several dormitories or dining rooms if they were free to choose the ratios of men and women that they prefer to live with? At Harvard in the 1970s there were a dozen houses for a population one-third women. A quite limited set of possibilities is consistent with these numbers. Four houses could be filled with women, eight with men. Twelve houses could be one-third women. Eight houses could be half and half with the other four all men. One house could be for women, four half and half, three houses two to one, and four all men. And so forth.

Insight can be obtained even by supposing only two houses. Make it dining halls rather than sleeping quarters, and suppose either hall can hold most of the population if packed in tightly. How will the men and women distribute themselves between the two dining halls if they are free to choose between the male-female ratios in these two locations.

In the easiest case, all the men and all the women prefer a one to one ratio and will choose the dining room in which the numbers are most nearly equal. Suppose that there are 120 women and 100 men, that the women have to choose in advance, and that everybody knows that everybody prefers 50–50.

The women expect the men to distribute themselves proportionately to the women in the two dining rooms, and, if the women don't like overcrowding, they distribute themselves equally between the two rooms.

Now the men arrive, and by the time three-quarters of them have arrived there may be 40 in one hall and 35 in the other. The later arrivals notice a slight discrepancy and choose the dining room with the more nearly equal number. In one room there are 60 women and 40 men, and in the other 60 and 35. The room with 40 men is slightly more attractive, and the next arrivals go there, and now there are 50 men in that room, 35 in the other. The difference is now more noticeable, and the next 10 men enter the hall with more men and there are 60 men and 60 women in that one, 35 men and 60 women in the other. The last 5 men much prefer the room with more men, and they make it 60 to 65 in that room, leaving it 60 to 35 in the other.

If men in the other room are now free to change their minds, maybe 10 of them will consider it worth the trouble to get up and change rooms, the near equality in the other room being appreciably better than the almost 1:2 ratio where they are. When the 10 arrive in the other room they change the ratio there to 75:60, spoiling the near equality, but leaving it 25:60 in the room they left, where some more men, now outnumbered nearly 3:1, prefer to go where the ratio is 5:4. Another 15 change rooms, leaving behind 10 men at a ratio of 6:1, making it 90:60 in the crowded room. Three to two is better than 6 to 1, so the last 10 go to the crowded room, raising the ratio there to 100:60.

The final score: all the men, preferring 50:50, have achieved 100:60. Half the women are outnumbered 1.6 to 1 and the other half will dine without men. No man will move.

If we forceably moved 40 men to the all-woman dining hall, *all* the men would enjoy a more satisfactory ratio, and so would all the women. But the 40 won't stay: the room with more men is always more attractive, even though both become less attractive as men migrate to the more attractive ratio.

At last the women committed to the dining room in which there are no men will insist on moving too, and everybody ends up in a very crowded room.

This quick illustration—an example, incidentally, of "equilibrium analysis"—is not for drawing conclusions. It is here to stimulate curiosity. Because association and proximity—in resi-

dence or social gatherings or working places, even marriage—
are such pervasive phenomena, in later chapters we explore
processes by which people become mixed or separated in
accordance with age, income, sex, race, or language.

Marriage has been discussed as an example of the phenomena we are discussing, but some additional dimensions are
worth mentioning. Age at marriage, and age differences
between spouses, are affected by the ages at which others
marry. Divorce and the prospects of remarriage depend on
whether there is a high rate of turnover in particular age
brackets. Especially if divorced people are likely to marry
divorced people, a high divorce rate can make divorce more
promising.

Language is an almost completely adaptive behavior. What
language a person speaks depends on what languages he
encounters, particularly within his own family. But the concentration and dispersion of languages in bilingual or linguisti-
cally separated countries like Canada, Finland, Switzerland,
and earlier Israel or the United States, display trends that,
though somewhat guided and sanctioned and stimulated by
schools, government, broadcasting and signposting, result from
individual decision and response. Accent, grammar and vocabulary are even more individualist in origin, slang being an outstanding example.

Each academic profession can study the development of its
own language. Some terms catch on and some don't. A hastily
chosen term that helps to meet a need gets imitated into the
language before anybody notices what an inappropriate term
it is. People who recognize that a term is a poor one use it
anyway in a hurry to save thinking of a better one, and in
collective laziness we let inappropriate terminology into our
language by default. Terms that once had accurate meanings
become popular, become carelessly used, and cease to communicate with accuracy. Sometimes a nugget is discovered, a
word freighted with just the right set of meanings to meet a
real need and to be popularly elected into the vocabulary. I

invite you to read on with an ear alert for examples of the good, the bad, and the ugly.

Like language are the communication systems that develop out of the unmanaged behaviors of individuals—the diffusion of rumor, gossip, and news, information and misinformation about sex and cooking and gardening and automobile repair; the circulation of jokes and stories and folklore; and the rules for playing games and adjudicating disputes. Everybody who participates in a communication system is part of the system. His participation maintains it or repairs it or transforms it or, sometimes, helps to cause it to wither away or collapse. People who pass along tips on the stock market or the horse races, where-to-get-it-wholesale, what movies to see or what restaurants to patronize, how to avoid getting caught, whom to date, and where to go for help, are simultaneously involved in two related activities. They are transmitting particular information over the network; and they are exercising the network.

Information networks, racial separation, marital behavior, and language development are often overlapping and interlocking. It is commonly observed that the work force of a shop or store or taxi company or motel is homogeneous. Whether it is Irish or Italian, Cuban or Puerto Rican, black or white, Protestant or Catholic, the homogeneity suggests purpose or design. But the determinant is likely to be a communication network. Positions are filled by people who learn of openings; people learn of the openings from acquaintances who already work there; acquaintances are from the same schools and neighborhoods and families and churches and clubs. And, the nearest thing to a guarantee that a new employee can have is an older employee who vouches for him.

I cannot resist digressing to describe an instance of segregation in which I used to participate. On birthdays I occasionally took a group of youngsters to watch the Red Sox. The second or third time I noticed, and confirmed the fourth and fifth time, that I sat in a section full of people who were remarkably like us—in their colors, accents, behavior, and dress. There was no overt segregation. The seats cost the same, so I wasn't sitting among people who could afford the seats I could afford. There were ten ticket windows, and the lines at all the windows were a mixture of young and old, black and white, male and female, well-dressed and poorly dressed, noisy and quiet. Why did we always end up sitting among people like us?

It was years before I learned the answer. Birthday parties require coordination, so I bought seats in advance. I bought them at the Harvard Square subway station. Most people want seats together, and the ticket agent will have fewer odd tickets left over if he gets a block of seats to begin with. So I sat with the people who bought tickets from the same block—with the people who bought seats in advance at Harvard Square. (My story stops there, but there are exciting tales of people whose romances got started because they used the same Laundromat.)

To continue with our listing, the subject includes systems of deference, etiquette, social status, and hierarchy. It includes "street behavior"—being on the streets or staying off; staring ahead or nodding hello; asking for directions, matches, the time of day, or spare change; and carrying weapons. It includes the formation of mobs and riots, panic behavior, rules of the road, traffic conventions, and the signals and insignia by which people recognize each other. It includes style and taste, hairstyles and cosmetics, clothing styles and jewelry, patterns of eating and drinking, coffee breaks and cocktail hours, tobacco, marijuana, littering and jaywalking, obeying and disobeying the law, and coming or not coming to help if somebody is in distress.

I want to avoid any suggestion that there is some single mechanism that underlies all of these behaviors. Quite the contrary. In some cases people want to conform, in others they want to be different. Sometimes there is immunity in numbers —jaywalking or smoking marijuana or double-parking (the police cannot afford to ticket all the illegally parked cars if there are many of them)—and other times too large a crowd spoils the fun. Sometimes people need to share a clandestine activity, and the outcome depends on whether there are penalties for revealing yourself to a stranger. Sometimes people want to associate with others who are older or richer or higher-ranked or who play better bridge or tennis; in other circumstances people are comfortable being older or richer or better; and sometimes the best is to be right in the middle. If everybody wants to stay home and watch the crowds in Times Square on television there will be no crowds in Times Square, while if everybody wants to join the crowd to be seen on television there will be nobody watching.

In the next chapter we examine a special class, an especially interesting class, of behavior patterns. These are patterns that have the characteristic of tending to be realized in the aggregate no matter how the individuals behave who comprise the aggregates. Musical chairs is an example: no matter how alert and aggressive the children are, one will be left chairless when the music stops. Poker is another: winnings and losings add to zero (less what one must pay for sandwiches) no matter how shrewdly people play their cards. Any one of us can get rid of Canadian quarters by passing them on, but collectively we cannot. A tenth of the students are always at the bottom 10 percent. And if you add up all the white neighbors of every black person in Boston, and add up the black neighbors of every white person in Boston, the numbers are identical as long as you are careful to use the same definitions of "neighbor," "Boston," "black," and "white," and to take both counts at the same time.

In Chapter 3 we shall look at a half dozen common models of behavior that social scientists use for insight into some of these processes. The number of different mechanisms is large but many recur repeatedly in widely different areas of activity. Some of these recurring models have proper names (reflecting the "naming phenomenon" I discussed earlier): "self-fulfilling prophecy," "critical mass," "the commons," "the market for lemons," the "acceleration principle." My purpose in leading you into this subject will be clearer, if it is not transparent yet, after I have done my best in Chapter 3 to demonstrate the usefulness of some of the models that have been developed for exploring this rich and complicated subject.

Chapters 4 and 5 will then illustrate this mode of analysis in some detail by examining processes of "sorting and mixing," segregation and integration. Hardly any choices are as interactive and interdependent as the choice of whom to associate with, live with, work with, or play with, eat with or drink with or sit beside. Chapter 4 focuses on discrete classifications like race, color, sex, or language; Chapter 5 deals with classification by "continuous" variables, like age, income, or level of skill. Chapter 6 then looks at a set of choices that is not quite available yet, choices that may become available and may be drastically interdependent—like choosing the sex of one's children.

Finally, and more rigorously, Chapter 7 shows how some formal theory can be built on these ideas. It is a more demanding chapter than the others, slower to read, less readily comprehended. Like reading blueprints, reading the diagrams of that chapter can be mastered by almost anyone but only by working at it. I know no easier way to gain access to this richly variegated and universally significant subject. I hope the earlier chapters will have stirred the interest needed to attack and conquer the last one. Through most of the first six chapters, possibly excepting some diagrams toward the end of Chapter 4 and a little elementary algebra that shows up in Chapter 5, it should be possible to move right along, pausing occasionally, but more to reflect than to study. If you read Chapter 7 thinking it should be instantly transparent you will only become discouraged. Reading diagrams is a little like learning a language; fluency comes only with practice. Readers familiar with diagrammatic analysis from economics and elsewhere will still have to pause over the diagrams of Chapter 7; readers not so used to diagrams will have to pause a little longer. Just knowing that most of Chapter 7 is not meant to be instantly obvious is probably all the help you need.

2

THE INESCAPABLE
MATHEMATICS
OF MUSICAL CHAIRS

TYPICAL OF ACTIVITIES in which one person's behavior influences another's is telephoning. One call leads to another. It may lead to a return call; or somebody learns something worth passing on; or a call initiates some business. Anyone who reads this can remember receiving a call in the last few days that stimulated one or more calls in response.

The behavior could be studied, and we would undoubtedly find that some people's phoning is highly responsive to calls they receive and other people's telephone lives are quite independent. Some make far more calls than they receive and others receive more than they make. We could classify people according to the ratio of calls made to calls received.

We can also calculate this ratio for the country as a whole (eliminating international calls, as we can't get the data we need from people at the other end of the line). Subject to a few ambiguities that we ought to clarify in defining "calls made" and "calls received," there are two considerations that make this an easy ratio to obtain. One is that the phone company may keep records. The second is that we don't need any data from the phone company. While none of us, except by coincidence, ever makes just as many calls as he happens to receive, together we make exactly as many.

We have to be careful to count wrong numbers either as calls received or as calls not made. Christmas calls to grandparents have to be counted as one call, or several, uniformly at both ends. A call transferred between extensions has to be counted once, or twice, but not differently at both ends. But if we clean up our definitions, all of us in a closed system make together exactly as many calls as we receive.

Christmas cards show the same phenomenon, although differently motivated, mainly stimulating cards in return. (I occasionally phone for taxis but taxis never phone me; most of the people to whom I send cards send cards to me—though I usually cannot remember who started it.) Some cards are unrequited, and some of us receive cards from people to whom we neglected, or refused, to send any. Some send more than we receive and some receive more than we send. If we ask which is more common, the card sent to an unrequiting addressee or the card received unexpectedly from somebody not on our list, the answer differs from person to person but for everybody within our postal system the two have to be identically frequent. Every unreciprocated card was *sent* unrequited by somebody and *received* unacknowledged by somebody else.

It is hard to find awesome significance in the way people respond to phone calls and Christmas cards. The excuse for beginning a chapter in this fashion is that some important kinds of behavior share this feature, and the feature is more readily apprehended in the familiar context of telephone connections. Actually it would be wrong to say it is characteristic of telephone *behavior* that calls received equal the calls placed—wrong because the observation has nothing to do with behavior. No matter how people behave—whether they refuse to answer the phone, never call on Sunday, promise to call back but never do, pass along every bit of gossip to somebody else— and no matter how many people dispatch taxis and ambulances on incoming calls or organize elections by calling five people who call five others, *together* we receive just as many calls as we place. It has nothing to do with behavior.

It has to do with the structure of telephone calls: each well-defined call has a sender and a receiver. ("Well-defined" for this purpose means only defined to exclude any disparity. For other purposes, like planning telephone extensions, other definitions would make more sense and lead to different numerical results.) Making a call is different from receiving one; for billing purposes a "call placed" is not the same as a "call received"; but an ideal recording system would record each call in a double-entry system, with a score in each column, so that the "operational definition" by which the two events are counted would be the same.

This telephone example is an instance of an important class of statements: propositions that are true in the aggregate but not in detail, and true independently of how people behave. They are true of the closed *system* of behavior but not of the behavior of each person nor even, necessarily, of any groups smaller than the whole population. Some of these propositions are obvious enough not to need pointing out. It would not surprise you that in Boston the number of left sneakers size 8½ is very nearly identical to the number of right sneakers the same size. It is only slightly less obvious that for the United States as a whole the number of people riding stolen bicycles is close to the number of people who have had bicycles stolen. (By identifying the discrepancies, like stolen bikes in transit, bikes damaged while stolen or worn out afterwards, and stolen bikes stolen again, we can make the statement more precise.)

Of the social sciences, economics is one in which this class of generalizations plays a central role. The reason is easy to see: economics is mainly concerned with exchanges of equivalent values. If I buy a bicycle I gain a bike and lose $150; the shop loses a bike and gains $150. The shop furthermore allocates $90 to the wholesale price of a replacement, $40 to rent, wages, and electricity, and $20 as earnings to the bike shop. If we trace the $90-bicycle bought wholesale, it decomposes in turn into parts for assembly, wages at the assembly shop, rent and electricity, and so forth. And the electricity goes into fuel, wages, interest on the generating plant, dividends, and taxes. And so forth. When we trace it all through we find that the earnings deriving from the $150 I spent on the bicycle, inclusive of income and profits and payroll taxes, have to add up to the $150.

Just why the earnings "have to" add up to $150, and just what definitions of earnings and taxes are pertinent to this important numerical statement, may not be obvious unless you have studied national-income accounting. I hope it is not quite obvious because my point is that many of these propositions are by no means obvious at first glance. And some not at second glance.

In economics these "accounting statements" are fundamental to the analysis of income and growth, money and credit, inflation, the balance of payments, capital markets, and public debt. They are frequently not obvious, especially not to the people who engage in the activities (rather than those who gather data in an analytical framework). The situation is like a game of musical chairs in which there are many players and chairs in different rooms, people play individually and in teams, the chairs removed are not readily observed, and sometimes new players and new chairs are added. Every player knows only that unless he's quick he'll be evicted for failing to sit when the music stops. Players become impatient with others who move slowly, while all the time you and I know that the number of chairs is smaller than the number of players and no matter how they play there is going to be some number of players left standing when the music stops, a number unaffected by how aggressively everybody plays. If we keep adding new players equal to the number evicted, replenishing players rather than removing chairs, we can calculate the average number of rounds that anybody will get to play before being caught chairless and evicted. The average is mathematically predetermined no matter who plays so well he stays forever or who loses out the first time around.

What we typically deal with in economics, as in much of the social sciences, is a feedback system. And the feedback "loop" is typically one of these relations that holds no matter how people behave. An output of one part of the system is an input to another part. We cannot all get rich by not spending our money, any more than at Christmastime we can all receive more value than we give by spending less on each other's presents.

Sometimes it appears that propositions as straightforward as the one about the Christmas cards can be forgotten, as when a day on the stock exchange is described as a day of great "selling" or great "buying." There is no known way to sell a share of stock—even a share you do not possess—except to somebody who buys it. And no way to buy except from somebody who sells. The people who refer to a selling wave mean something; but it is occasionally necessary to remind ourselves there can be no "wave" of selling unless there is equivalent buying, whether we call it a "wave" or not.

Defining the Terms

I shall shortly get on with more of these propositions about "behavior" that are independent of the way people behave, and show that they can be helpful in thinking about the way people marry and have children, live and work and migrate and retire. But first some discussion of the status of these propositions is worthwhile.

Notice that, as I have described them or at least anticipated those to be described, they have something of the character of a truism or of what, in mathematics, might be called an "identical equation." An identical equation is one that holds irrespective of numerical values. The statement, $(a + b)(a - b) = a^2 - b^2$, is not an equation that we solve for the values of a and b that make it true; it is true for any values of a and b. It is an unconditional statement. We do not demonstrate its truth by trying a sample of numbers; either side of the equation can be derived from the other by standard operations. Comparable verbal statements are often said to be "true by definition," or, more accurately, derivable from definitions, axioms and assumptions, by logical operations.

It is sometimes implied that any proposition that is true by definition—inherently true irrespective of what the facts may be, compatible with all possible facts—does not give any information. To say that the cubic footage of housing space in the United States is equal to the square footage multiplied by the mean height of the ceilings, cannot do much more than remind us of the definition of cubic footage.

And there is a respect in which propositions of the kind I

am discussing are dependent on their definitions. But it is a respect in which almost any proposition is dependent on definitions, including those that have to be established by reference to empirical data. Consider the statement that, on the average, the larger the income of an urban family the smaller the fraction spent on housing. This proposition, if true, is not "true by definition." But its truth *is* dependent on the way "income," "housing," and "urban family" are defined, especially if the statement is put in numerical form. We have to define whether "housing" includes the main domicile or vacation housing, nights in hotels, college dormitories, garages; whether it includes land or just buildings, utilities or just the housing, family-occupied housing or sublet rooms. For owner-occupied houses, the definition must specify whether "expenditure" includes real-estate taxes and a hypothetical amount equivalent to the rental value of the property; and "income" must be defined to include or exclude the "rent" the family hypothetically pays itself and any capital appreciation. The definition has to be careful to stipulate whether working children living at home, and grandparents, are part of the "family," and whether the grandparents' retirement annuities are "income." And so forth. In general, the better the definition, the truer the proposition. Since the purpose is to find interesting regularities of behavior, "better" definitions will be those that yield statistically valid propositions.

But there will be another proposition, one belonging to the class considered in this chapter, stating that housing expenditures of urban families equal the gross incomes earned in the provision of housing to urban families. This statement will also be more nearly true, the more careful we are to define "gross income" in a way that corresponds to an exhaustive division, by ultimate recipients and claimants, of the receipts corresponding to those housing expenditures. If our definitions neglect maintenance expenditure or local government's "income" in real-estate taxes, or exclude electricity from gross income while including it in expenditures, our proposition will not be true. (Similarly, our proposition about telephone calls was not going to be true if every call for the recorded weather is treated as made but not received.)

Both kinds of propositions depend crucially on defining terms appropriately on both sides of the equation. The difference is that in the one case the two sides of the equation, or the two terms of the proposition, are under no logical compulsion to display the asserted relationship—housing expenditure as a percentage could just as well go up as down, when income rises—while in the other case the truth of the proposition depends solely on the exhaustiveness with which we have identified all possibilities and allowed for them in the terms of the proposition. Similarly, the statement that the percent allocated to everything else must go down if the percent allocated to housing goes up, need not be established by counting expenditures on food, entertainment, taxes, and savings bonds. It has to be true for the same reason that if tuberculosis diminishes as a cause of death, other causes together must increase, as long as we impute a cause to every death.

The question is whether these propositions, though their validity depends on whether we have defined our terms with enough care to make them true, tell us anything we didn't know, or tell somebody else—somebody who didn't struggle with the definition to make the propositions true—something he or she didn't know. On this, everybody can be his own judge. If it tells you something you didn't know, or that hadn't occurred to you, you're ahead. Then the proposition tells you something about the world, though it will not count as an empirically-established scientific generalization. If it never occurred to you that one of the reasons why proportionately more people today die from *non-infectious* diseases than they did fifty years ago is that deaths from *infectious* diseases have declined, and not necessarily because of any change in the lethality of the other ailments, you're ahead for having it called to your attention, even if you do feel a little silly that the point originally escaped you.

Many puzzles have the appearance of not containing enough data to permit a solution, but turn out to hinge on one of these identities that was not quite obvious. (What makes the puzzle interesting is usually how "obvious" the point is after you tumble to it.) You have a glass of gin and a glass of vermouth. You lift a tablespoonful of gin and pour it into the vermouth. You then take a tablespoonful of the liquid in the second glass, vermouth with some gin in it, and transfer it to the first glass. Which now is the greater quantity, vermouth in the gin glass or gin in the vermouth glass?

A man in a rowboat drops his corked bottle overboard and rows upstream half an hour before discovering his bottle is missing; he turns about and rows downstream at the same pace until he overtakes the bottle just before the current carries it over the dam. The current is two miles an hour. How far above the dam did the bottle fall overboard?

You have a floor 16 feet square to cover with tiles 2 feet by 1. It would take 128 tiles, but you want to leave uncovered a square foot at the northeast corner and another at the southwest corner, to accommodate heating and electrical outlets. As the 2 square feet to be left blank are equivalent to one tile, 127 tiles ought to do the job but they cannot be laid in parallel rows end to end. What is the pattern in which the tiles must be laid, or can it not be done?

For those among you to whom the solutions are not obvious, even after a little reflection, there's a note at the end of the chapter. Experience shows you are not alone. The proposition about telephone calls with which the chapter started is not always obvious, and if one specializes it to pertain, say, to long-distance calls between people of opposite sex, it becomes even less obvious. Millions of hours of teaching suggest that some of the most fundamental "accounting identities" in economics are not obvious to begin with and not even obvious upon being stated, and have to be worked through with care before a student sees them the way he sees that winnings have to equal losings in a poker game, or that we cannot all get rid of our Canadian quarters by passing them along quickly to each other.

There's a reason why many of these propositions are not obvious. They do not correspond to anything in the experience of the person who does the things that the proposition is about. The person who on the same day pays an overdue insurance premium, makes final payment on a bank loan, and pays the final installment on a color TV, is not likely to know which of these transactions reduced the money supply of the United States of America. More interesting, neither his banker nor his TV salesman is likely to know either. The student who selects a college or a course load with a view to being in the upper half of his class, or the customer who likes to tip his barber a little above the average, needn't bother himself with what would happen if everybody tried to do the same. Some people still haven't worked out how many couples can be seated at a rectangular table so that sexes alternate, no spouses are side by side, and host and hostess are at opposite ends of the table. And it may not have occurred to most people, even those who cater weddings, that if men marry women four years younger in a population that has been growing at 3 percent per year, women of marrying age may outnumber men by more than 12 percent. Most people think that inflation reduces purchasing power without stopping to notice that their own pay increases are somebody else's inflation, and at least some of it must cancel out.

The propositions tend to be true only in the aggregate, or only when both sides of two-party transactions are taken into account. The citizen's experience is with one side of a transaction, or with situations in which if you hurry a little you'll be ahead of somebody else. There are still toll bridges and turnpikes on which nearly all the cars, six days a week, go back and forth but tolls are collected in both directions, at twice the cost and twice the traffic delay.

Pairing from Two Populations

When pairs are formed from complementary populations there are some ineluctable mathematics. Marriage is the outstanding example, and monogamy has in its favor that, in a natural population with similar numbers of men and women and not too dissimilar life expectancies, it is an arrangement compatible with a high incidence of marriage and equal opportunity for both sexes.

A fact of some significance is that in a monogamous population the difference between the number of unmarried women and unmarried men is the same as the difference between women and men. And if we count the women and men over some common age of eligibility for marriage, the percentage difference between the two in a stable population will be the percentage difference in life expectancies at that age.[1] If women live longer or marry earlier there will be more women than men. There will be (the same number) more unmarried women than unmarried men. And the ratio of unmarried women to unmarried men will be larger, the more people are married. If women begin to marry at seventeen and (as in the United States) have a life expectancy of another sixty years, and men at twenty-one with a remaining life expectancy of fifty, in a stationary population adult women will exceed men in the ratio of 60:50. If one-fifth of the men are unmarried, one-third of the women will be. If women marry three years earlier and live seven years longer than men, women will average ten years longer divorced or widowed than men.

It has been suggested that marriage customs are out of phase with life expectancies, women living longer and marrying younger with a prospect of long widowhood. It is not evi-

---

[1] Not quite. In the United States more boys are born than girls, in the ratio of 1:05; young males die more than young females, and by about age 25 the difference is less than 3 percent. So the exact statement is slightly more complex than the one in the text.

dent that either women or men would prefer it otherwise, but if they do we can consider the arithmetic of reducing the differential, or reversing it. Considering first marriages only in a constant population, suppose the average excess of husband's over wife's age were reduced to zero within a decade. Afterwards, everything is synchronized: men coming of age equal the women, and it should be as easy to find a partner as it used to be. But along the way there is going to be a mismatch equal to a three-year cohort. Men will marry younger, women will marry older, or both. If men marry younger, a thirteen-year cohort will become marriageable within the ten years with no change in the number of women; an extra three years' supply of men goes unmarried. If women marry three years older, a seven-years' supply of women becomes marriageable during the decade, with a ten-years' supply of men, and still a three-years' supply of men goes unmarried. The same is true of any combination.

The arithmetic is not peculiar to marriage. It applies to any synchronized flow of two sets of objects or individuals, if there is a shift of phase.

In the marriage example, we begin with an excess of widows over widowers. So there *are* women to match the men. But if twenty-five-year-old men and seventy-year-old women don't suit each other, a hump in the age distribution of unmarried males will persist for a half century.

Not quite. If everybody married early and divorce were uncommon, this three-years' excess of men would be a lost generation (like women in countries where young men were decimated in war). But there is divorce, and not everybody marries initially, so there will be some unmarried women at every age. Some young men will marry older women and some older men will marry women even older because of this three-years' excess. Shifting the phase by three years will cause a three-years' supply of marriageable men to go unmarried *or* to marry older women. What cannot be done is to match the young men and the young women. There is a three-years' supply that has to make other arrangements, just as, when we finally go off daylight saving, there is an extra hour to be filled.

The arithmetic of paired populations applies equally to marriage across racial or linguistic lines. For characteristics that are homogeneous in the family, like race and language, the numbers of young men and women in some first-marriage age bracket will be about the same. If there is asymmetry between men and women in marrying across group lines—English-speaking men having more opportunity to marry French-speaking women, i.e., French-speaking women having more opportunity to marry English-speaking men—than the other way around, there will be an excess of unmarried women among the English-speaking, and an excess of unmarried men among French-speaking, *no matter how many people get married*. (Military forces overseas is an example.)

Taking all the cross-group marriages together, we have it true by definition (for monogamous marriage and populations exhaustively divided between white and black) that the percentages of whites married to blacks and of blacks married to whites are in inverse ratio to the populations. So in the United States the percentage of blacks married to whites in this generation will be about eight times the percentage of whites married to blacks, no matter how many whites and blacks marry each other.

Distributive Ratios among Two Populations

Marriage is a special case. We are often interested in the ratios of two populations in several locations. An example is a dozen dormitories and a college population three-quarters male. Lots of combinations are possible, all subject to one numerical constraint. There is, for example, a unique ratio that can be common to all the dormitories: 3 to 1. There is a unique way to divide the men and women so that all women live in dormitories that are half men: six may be half and half, the other six all men. If two dormitories are women only, the ratios in the other ten must average 9 to 1. Exactly two houses can be half and half if two houses are all women. And so forth. The principle holds for freshmen, black students, married students or any other group. If black students are one-twelfth of the college they can be all in one dormitory, 50–50 in two dormitories, or 1 to 3 in four dorms. There is no way to get whites living, on the average, with more than one black student out of twelve.

On a smaller scale, the indivisibility of people becomes important. Distributed among four-person rooms nobody can be less than 25 percent of his local population. If blacks are a twelfth of the total, only three-elevenths of the whites can have any black roommates at all. If every black prefers one black roommate, and if whites feel the same, the only acceptable ratio will be two and two, with ten-twelfths of the rooms in the college being white only. The same applies to hospital wards, military squads, and, in the extreme case, pairs of police in two-man squad cars where all integrated cars are 50–50 and nobody in an integrated car is with anybody his own color.

If you find it hard to believe that anybody can fail to master this unexciting arithmetic, I have to assert that people are indeed able to be unaware of it (even though it may seem so obvious that one doesn't need to "know it" to take it into account). Considering how banal these propositions sound, it is astonishing how many hours of committee meetings have been spent on proposals to mix men and women in dormitories, or blacks and whites, or freshmen and sophomores, in ways that violated the simple arithmetic principle that no matter how you distribute them, the numbers in all the dormitories have to add up to the numbers that there are.

The Dynamics of Aging

Demography is interlaced with inviolable quantitative relations. Many have to do with the simple fact that everybody who survives a year becomes a year older. Last year's 20-year-olds, less those who died, are this year's 21-year-olds. There is only one way to make a 22-year-old out of a 21-year-old: wait a year.

We saw a special case in the marrying ages of two sychronized populations, with a shift in their phasing; similar phenomena arise with a single population.[2]

Consider what happens when the age of entry to some activity is shifted a year or two. An example is the induction age for draftees into the army, or the age for entering first grade, or adding a year to high school or subtracting a year.

Consider two million men in the army, drafted the year they become twenty-one and serving two years, and a new decision to take draftees in their twentieth year. There are three possibilities.

We can skip a year's class. Until the change, everybody is vulnerable in a particular year of his life; after the change, everybody is vulnerable in a particular year of his life; the year of the change is a year of jubilee—men who become twenty-one are skipped by the draft and save two years of their civilian lives.

Or we can induct a two-years' supply in a single year and have an army of three million for two years. Or the 20-year-olds and the 21-year-olds can be drafted together while the 22-year-olds are discharged a year early; and next year half the draftees with a year's service are discharged.

In other words, a million skip two years' service; two million skip a year apiece; or, an extra million are in the army for two years.

It is like daylight saving going into effect at a hockey rink that has people signed up every hour around the clock. The youngsters who reserved from midnight to 1:00 show up at

[2] An interesting and, at first glance, puzzling statistic occurs from the dynamics of population growth. At present U.S. mortality rates, 25 percent die before they reach 65, and more than one-third of those who die are younger than 65. The discrepancy follows from population growth. Suppose 25 percent die at 50, 75 percent at 75, and births increase at 2 percent per year. For every 100 born 75 years ago 75 die this year; and for every 100 born 75 years ago $100 \times (1.02)^{25}$ or 164 were born 50 years ago, 25 percent of whom, or 41, die this year. So 116 die this year, of whom 35 percent are 50.

11:45, put on their skates, and in fifteen minutes it's 1:00 and their hour has "passed." Or they can double up with the kids who reserved from 1:00 to 2:00, or split the rink thirty minutes apiece. The wheels turn at the same rate, but slipping a cog causes a once-for-all overlap of demand and supply.

In the same way, if the draft age is raised we can cut the army by a million men for two years, keep two classes for three years instead of two, or draft a million men from somewhere else. Arithmetically it can't be otherwise.

Notice the relation among our three variables: the rate of induction, the term of service, and the size of the population. If two million reach draft age every year and you want all to serve equally, and you want two million in the army, you must keep them for exactly one year. If you want two million in the army and every draftee to serve two years, you can draft only one million: half serve and half don't. If you want to draft two million a year, for two years each, with two million in the army, you'll have to invent a new arithmetic.

The same kind of arithmetic governs the relation between, say, clearing the court's calendar by more expeditious processing of criminal charges—prisons will be more crowded for a period equal to the average term served, or there will have to be more acquittals, or prisoners will have to be paroled sooner. Waiting lines for hospital beds show the same phenomenon.

And if "zero-population-growth" went into effect at once, by holding new births equal to normal deaths, the portion of the population under twenty-five would be down from the present 43 percent to half that—22 percent—by the year 2000, and would then rise gradually toward 33 percent if the present age-specific mortality went unchanged.

The Acceleration Principle

I have a friend who likes to chop firewood. He likes it the way people like to hit tennis balls. The trouble is that he can't chop firewood without getting firewood.

He also burns wood, but there is no relation between the

amount he likes to chop and the amount he burns. The two activities are unrelated, except that one happens to produce fuel and the other happens to consume it. He likes to chop much more than he will ever burn. He can't throw it away; the fun disappears if he admits he is simply breaking up sticks for faster rotting. He can't sell it and he can't give it away.

I have friends who love small children. They like teenagers too, but they especially like small children. Small ones become big ones and they don't want that many big ones. If little children could take 15 years to reach the age of 7, these friends could be satisfied with two or three children. But if they are always going to have a couple of children under 7 for the next 20 years or so, they are going to have bigger families than they can support.

Housing construction is important, and not only because it happens to replenish and add to the stock of housing. It is what a lot of people do for a living. It draws on industries like cement and lumber, paint and plumbing; and it is important to the people who sell automobiles and baseball tickets to the people who make a living by building houses. But housing is durable stuff. What happens to the construction industry if it is decided to increase housing by 25 percent in five years? The industry has been replacing 1 percent of the housing every year and supporting growth of 2½ percent. The stock of housing is now to grow at 5 percent; the industry, to produce the equivalent of 6 percent rather than 3½ percent, must nearly double, hold there for five years, and fall back to a new "normal" production rate again. For the stock of housing to grow by an extra 2½ percent per year, the construction industry must expand instantly by nearly 100 percent; and five years later, when the housing stock resumes growing at 2½ percent, the construction industry actually will contract.

The same applies to minority recruitment. Suppose turnover in some labor supply is 5 percent per year—say, postal employees. The percentage of black employees has been a steady 5 percent of a half million workers, or 25,000, and normal recruitment is 1,250 blacks and 23,750 whites per year. Now it is decided to increase blacks from 5 to 11 percent in four years. During four years the number of blacks must increase by 30,000 while 5,000 quit or retire; 35,000 must be recruited while total recruitment is 100,000. The percentage of blacks among the recruits jumps from 5 to 35, sevenfold, and drops to 11 at the end of four years.

Notice that if turnover were twice as large (and people averaged ten years on the job instead of twenty), annual recruitment would have been twice as large, recruitment during the four-year period would have been 200,000 and black recruitment 40,000, or a jump from 5 to 20 percent rather than 5 to 35. The "leverage" that a change in the steady level has on the recruitment rate varies with the longevity of the population, inversely with the turnover. If a four-year college is to raise the percentage of minority students from 5 to 15 percent, a quarter of the freshman must be minorities to do it in two years, 45 percent minorities to do it in one year.

The same principle applies to those two million draftees. They spend six months in training, so the Army has 1.5 million trained men. In an emergency it is decided to double the number of trained men and to do it in six months. We were inducting half a million every six months, training them for six months, and sending them out to replace men who had finished two years of service. Now we induct, during six months, the half million replacements plus 1.5 million. For six months we induct four times as many as we used to induct. By the middle of the year we are training four times as many as we used to train. If the tour of service remains two years, semi-annual inductions fall from 2 to .5 million at the end of the half year, and the number in training does too.

The principle can be compounded. Suppose inductees are trained by people who go through a two-month training course themselves; the ratio of trainers to trainees is 1 to 11; and the typical trainer (himself a draftee) stays twenty-two months in the job. To train a half million recruits requires about 45,000 trainers plus 4,000 at a time in training and 2,000 turnovers per month. When we double the army over a six-month period, and train four times as many new draftees, we need four times as many trainers: 180,000 instead of 45,000. And we need them right now. We put 137,000 new ones into a two-month training course that has been handling 4,000 at a time. The increase is nearly thirty-five fold! (My guess is that we won't.)

Again, the crucial variables are (1) the increase in the level of some stock or population, (2) the speed with which that increase is to occur, and (3) the durability or longevity, i.e., the rate of turnover to which the growth rate is added. In economics this is called the "acceleration principle." The acceleration principle is evidenced whenever two activities that are *independently* interesting are *dependently* related, by one's being the other's source of growth. (Production of jogging shoes would ordinarily be about proportionate to the *rate of sale* of jogging shoes—proportionate to jogging, if jogging were constant over time—but construction of additional jogging-shoe factories will more likely be proportionate to the *rate of increase* of the *rate of production*, the way "acceleration" is related to speed. Hence the name. In economics it is important in the quantitative relation between investment and consumption.) The principle is reflected in everybody's personal energy budget: eating and body weight are separately interesting but, the amount of one affecting the change in the other, inseparably related.

Positions in a Distribution

Ask people whether they consider themselves above or below average as drivers. Most people rank themselves above. When you tell them that, most of them smile sheepishly.

There are three possibilities. The average they have in mind is an arithmetic mean and if a minority drive badly enough a big majority can be "above average." Or everybody ranks himself high in qualities he values: careful drivers give weight to care, skillful drivers give weight to skill, and those who think that, whatever else they are not, at least they are polite, give weight to courtesy, and come out high on their own scale. (This is the way that every child has the best dog on the block.) Or some of us are kidding ourselves.

We can ask more specifically whether they consider themselves above or below the median in the care with which they drive; now if we catch many more than half of them in the upper half we ought to get a few sheepish smiles when we tell them the results (although they may just expect each other to smile sheepishly).

The fact is that 20 percent of the people are among the poorest 20 percent, 15 percent are among the tallest 15 percent, and 10 percent of college freshmen are in the bottom tenth of their class.

Actually it isn't a fact. It's a definition. It is a "fact" if the bottom 10 percent can be identified; it is a "fact" if there is some grade average that assigns everybody a percentile; it is a "fact" if the top ten batting averages during the first week of the season are of any lasting interest. It may even be a "fact" that the number of people who are the "single best all-round athlete in the United States" is exactly one—if sometimes nobody is so identified, and sometimes two people are tied. But it is only a definition that the tallest third are taller than the next third.

The statements continue to hold when the bottom tenth of the class or the youngest fifth among the elderly residents have withdrawn or dropped out or been expelled. You cannot get rid of the youngest fifth by getting rid of the youngest fifth!

More important "facts" are that in a lot of activities and situations it matters to people whether they are older or younger, poorer or richer, shorter or taller than others, and specifically whether they are in something like the bottom two-thirds or half or quarter or tenth. It matters in putting together a sandlot baseball team, subscribing elderly people in a residential home, joining a tennis club, or enrolling in a law school.

The statement that a fifth of the people will be in the youngest fifth is trivial as information but not in its implications. The statement, notice, is not true of anybody in particular. It is not about an individual. It is only about the composition of a group. It becomes a factual statement—a scientifically relevant, empirically verifiable statement—if we specify that people not only care but have some idea whether or not they are in that bottom 20 percent, or that they systematically perceive themselves a little younger or a little older, relative to the population, than they actually are. If nobody will stay in a tennis club in which 90 percent of the members play an inferior game, the club will unravel as everybody leaves in turn, the "best" becoming progressively worse. The speed with which it happens depends on whether only the top 2 percent or the top 15 percent believe themselves in the top 10, whether the best five among the top 10 percent leave in haste while the less outstanding take their time, and how quickly the satisfied people at the 80th percentile discover that the better players are quitting or have already gone.

Spatial relations, as in the auditorium with which we began this book, are a particular instance of this principle. Just as somebody is always the oldest, somebody is always in front. If all want to be in the center of a crowd they won't succeed, and if all want to be on the edge of the crowd they won't succeed and may not make a crowd. Their wishes are individually reasonable but collectively insatiable.

The principles apply to what people do as well as to what they are. Everybody may wish to tip a waiter a little more than average, to write a longer than average term paper, or not to bother arriving until most of the people are present. Each of these formulations, of course, can be expressed in terms of mean values and medians, upper thirds and lower quarters, and top 10 percents. At the extreme there may be no one willing to be the youngest or the shortest or the poorest, or to be the first —to stand up, to start clapping, to speak out, or to swim naked.

Waiting Lines and Through-Put Systems

Standing in line at a ski lift—a long line—I overheard somebody complain that the chairs ought to go faster. It would take a bigger engine, but at those fees the management could afford one. The complaint deserves sympathy but the proposal doesn't work: speeding the lift makes the lines longer.

We have a circulating system with a fixed population. Everybody repetitively makes the circuit, though not in the same order. It takes a pair of people a certain time, after the pair ahead has been lifted away, to get positioned for the next chair. The loading rate of two skiers in six seconds is independent of the speed of the chairs (although if the chairs moved faster it would be even more important to be properly positioned, and the interval should be lengthened slightly). Approximately twenty people per minute can load.

The population is divided into four locations: going up, coming down, standing in line, or taking time off in the warming hut. If time indoors is independent of the lift lines, we can analyze the population that circulates up the lift, down the slope, and through the line. If the loading rate is twenty per minute the unloading rate at the top is the same. And if people ski down at speeds unaffected by how fast they went up, the speed of the lift will not affect the number of people in the skiing phase. Subtracting that fixed component from the fixed total leaves unchanged the sum of the people in the two other phases. But the number in chairs is *reduced* when the lift speed increases; people enter the chairs at the same rate but sit a shorter time. (Chairs are spaced farther apart.) If the same number is coming down and a smaller number going up, more must be in the third place. And that's the line. Speeding the lift does not reduce delay, it reduces only the part spent sitting.

We have a similar experience commuting through successive traffic jams. Whenever we are averaging five miles per hour, starting and stopping until we pass through the bottleneck, we wish somebody would widen the road or eliminate left turns or repair the surface to speed the traffic. One morning to our delight the road has been widened and we sail through without reducing speed—right into the next line at the next narrow place. And so did everybody ahead of us. The line there is twice as long and all they did, by widening the first bottleneck, was to combine the lines at the next bottleneck.

What we have is a "conservative quantity." In physics and chemistry there are "principles of conservation," like the conservation of energy, mass, or momentum. If you launch a squash court into orbit the trajectory of its center of gravity will be undisturbed by the game being played inside. The internal activity cancels out. These principles of conservation in the physical sciences play the role that accounting systems do in economics. They *are* accounting systems—double-entry bookkeeping systems. In gambling we have the principle of "conservation of assets," according to which in the aggregate there is no gain or loss. In a weekend of bets on sporting events the winnings equal the losings. They do, that is, if we are careful, as physicists and chemists are careful, to keep track of all of the exceptions or "leakages" and record them in the accounts. If some of the pot in a poker game goes to the house we have to treat that as a "cost" and not a "loss" at poker. If the state taxes the game we must treat the state as a "winner" or count part of the losings as tax payments. In the same way, the conservation of energy in mechanical systems had to make allowance for loss due to friction; the books balance because friction produces heat equivalent, at a regular exchange rate, to the mechanical energy that disappears.

Our ski lift is a "conservative system." There are arrivals from the parking lot and departures before closing time, but if we make allowance for late arrivals and early departures, and for people in lunch lines and rest rooms, we have everybody in our accounting system. The three stages of our lift-line circuit —riding up, skiing down, and standing in line—make a semi-closed system. By "semi-closed" I mean a system that gains or loses the things we are keeping track of at a limited number of entry and exit points at which, if we wish, we can count them. (Almost anything *can* be considered a semi-closed system, even a busy intersection, but whether it is *useful* to construe it that way depends on whether the turnover is so large that it becomes silly to treat it as an almost-closed system.)

Migration is a semi-closed system. Any city or state can reduce the residents on welfare by excluding people who would be on welfare or inducing them to leave. But all states together cannot, except as people die or leave the country, and all cities together can do it only so long as frustrated migrants are on route between cities or assimilated into the countryside. A widely read book on urban policy proposed a decade ago that a city could raise its average income by not building low-income housing. People with low income would leave, not arrive, if housing were bad enough. The advice was the kind that any individual city could put into effect. But the success of one city is the failure of another, and together they succeed only if bad housing can somehow reduce the total number of urban poor. (It might—or it might not—but that was not part of the advice.)

Many populations circulate in semi-closed systems, and some display special patterns. The bridge across San Francisco Bay accommodates mainly people who travel one way in the morning and the other way in the afternoon. In winter, Interstate 93 in New Hampshire carries weekend traffic that travels first north, then south. The people go north at different times of day, but all go south in one big Sunday evening rush. The line at the toll booth is thirty minutes long. In San Francisco they charge you double one way and nothing the other; nearly everybody breaks even in money, all the drivers save time, the occasional traveler from Seattle to Los Angeles is stuck with a double toll and the one from Los Angeles to Seattle comes out twenty-five cents ahead, and collection costs are reduced. The New Hampshire highways haven't learned what the New Hampshire ski slopes learned long ago: if you can make people pay to go up the mountain you don't have to make them pay to come down. When the Highway 93 people tumble to their local conservation principle, let's hope they have enough sense to collect the double toll going northbound and not southbound.[3]

Other "populations" circulating within semi-closed systems are returnable bottles, Avis cars, and DDT. The proposal that every new car should be subject to a "disposal tax," to cover the ultimate cost of caring for the carcass, is a recognition that every car produced dies sooner or later and dies only once.

Systems of Leakage and Decay

In planning the logistics for a tennis tournament a person is lucky if the number of players is a power of 2, like 32 or 128. You need a can of balls for every game, and it is easy to count how many games need to be played. With 128 players you first play 64 matches, then half that many, then half again as many, and so on until the final match. But suppose 129 people sign up. Somebody is left out of the first round. He can join the second round but then somebody is left out of the third round. How many cans of balls do we need?

We don't need to do the arithmetic. Somebody observed that every match eliminates one person and the tournament is over when all but one have been eliminated. If there are 129 entrants, 128 must lose a match. No two people lose the same match, so it takes 128 matches to eliminate 128 people. We need 128 cans of balls. If instead of 129 we had 128, we might add $64 + 32 + 16 + 8 + \ldots$ and consider ourselves lucky it came out so neatly; if the problem is a little harder we are

---

[3] Let's hope they don't confuse that issue with another one: if traffic lights at successive intersections are synchronized for 35 mph going from east to west, will they also be synchronized for 35 going west to east?

motivated to find the formula that eliminates all this division by 2.

Similarly in calculating the incomes that accrue when a person buys a $195-water heater. We can estimate how much iron was mined and made into steel, how much oil was produced to power the railroads that carried the coke to the steel mill and the steel to the metal-fabricating plant, how many petrochemicals went into the nylon nozzle on the spraying device that painted the exterior of the finished heater, what the markup was at the wholesaler's and retailer's, and what the wage rates and productivity were in the plant that produced the glass liner, and what interest charges and real estate taxes were paid on all the plants along the way. We need all of that if we want to know where and to whom the incomes accrued. But if we want to know only how much income accrued, we have something like the tennis tournament. Subject to a few provisos, the incomes resulting from the expenditure ought to come to $195.

The original recipient of the $195 kept some and passed the rest along. Regardless of whether he passed it along as wages, interest, taxes, rent, or the purchase of a water heater wholesale, what he didn't keep as income he paid as "expenses." Each "expense" accrues to somebody who keeps part as income and passes the rest along as "expenses." Again, he can pass it along as taxes or wages or interest or delivery charges or the cost of raw materials or whatever it may be. The part that he does not keep as income he passes on. At the next stage somebody keeps some as income and passes the rest along. And so forth. It we follow the process until there is nothing left to pass along, the amounts taken out cannot add to more than $195 and, unless there's something we haven't traced to the end, cannot add up to less.

If somebody lost money on the transaction, he added something to pay more expenses than he got as receipts; if we treat that as negative income, the total is a "conservative quantity." Somebody may have used a can of paint that he had on hand, paying out no money; but his saving in expenses isn't quite "income," because he used assets worth money. We have a choice: we can count the income that did accrue at the time that he bought the paint; we can count the income that will accrue when he replenishes his can of paint; or, we can offset the $195-investment by the associated "disinvestment" that took the form of liquidation of inventory (paint). Even in the tennis tournament we have to make allowance for people who provide their own tennis balls.

A similar principle is involved in the puzzle: if the probability of male or female birth for every couple is 50 percent, what happens to the ratio of boy to girl children if every couple wants only a boy and completes the family at the first boy? Half the people will get boys at first birth and stop. Couples with girls will go on, stopping when they have a boy while others go on in hopes of a boy. How does this bias the ultimate ratio of boys to girls in the population? (It has occasionally been proposed that this motivation might explain a slight excess of boys over girls in some populations. Where female infanticide is practiced it is bound to have that result.)

Reflection makes clear that no "stopping rules," like stopping after the first boy, can affect the ultimate proportions. At the first round, half the babies will be boys. At the second round, only half the families have children, but they will be half boys. The half with only girls will proceed to the third round and again, by the 50–50 hypothesis, half will have boys and half girls. If at each round half are boys and half girls the total—no matter where it stops—will be half boys and half girls. (A corollary is that we know, without adding, how many children will be born. In the end, every family will have one boy; girls will equal boys; and, the average will be two children per family.)

Some similar principles show up in genetics. If a recessive gene is lethal early in life when paired with the same gene and has no effect otherwise on anything related to ultimate reproduction, in a stable population the number of deaths ultimately required to eliminate the gene from the population is equal to half the number of such genes. The requirement is independent of how the gene is distributed among intermarrying groups. And in a growing population a corresponding but more complicated statement holds.

Pattern and Structure

Enough examples have been given to suggest the frequency, if not the ubiquity, of these patterns and structures that underlie many of the numbers and quantities we deal with in the social sciences. These patterns and structures impose a certain discipline on the variables, reducing the "degrees of freedom" that related activities can enjoy, limiting the arrangements and outcomes that are mathematically possible, and making some equivalences hold among events or activities or distributions that appear at first glance to be more independent of each other than they turn out to be.

It would be helpful to have a logical scheme or exhaustive taxonomy for all of these closed systems, conservative quantities, paired events, reciprocal flows, accounting statements and transition matrices, and theorems based on symmetries and reciprocities or derived purely from the definitions of transactions. But I know of none, and would not be sure where to draw the line if I did.

People concerned with climate and energy have to work with the principle that all the carbon in the atmosphere, the oceans, the living and dead vegetation, and the fossil fuels yet to be burned, is an almost-fixed quantity in an almost-closed system (some coming out of volcanoes and some going into rocks); the carbon dioxide caused by decaying, burning, and metabolizing vegetation may be recycled through new vegetation, but what comes from burning oil and coal is a net addition to the atmosphere, except for what dissolves in the oceans or goes into any enlarged mass of total vegetation. And in the atmosphere it affects the earth's solar-energy balance. Whether you consider carbon dioxide to be chemistry, geology, or climatology, it is a crucial part of our environment that displays a principle of conservation that we see in other situations: we cannot get rid of mercury by dumping it in a river, we cannot get rid of the elderly by moving them to another state, and we cannot get rid of disfigured coins by spending them as rapidly as we receive them.

The "carbon dioxide budget" intersects another conservative system, the "energy budget," according to which the solar energy that strikes the earth must all be reflected back into space, chemically preserved in vegetation through photosynthesis, absorbed in evaporation or in the melting of snow and ice, or used to warm the atmosphere, the oceans, and the earth's crust. Even the solar energy "collected" and transformed into electricity in the southwestern desert, then used to charge storage batteries that will power electric automobiles in the east, will be released again to the atmosphere, like the energy stored in a grain of rice; and windmills not only generate electricity but slow down the winds, transforming one kind of potential energy into another.

Intersecting the energy budget is the earth's "water budget," according to which all the water is cycling among the oceans, lakes, rivers, and streams, icecaps and snow covers, clouds and humidity, raindrops, plant moisture, wet soil, subsoil water tables, and animal bodies, or cycling through the hydrocarbons (and a little free hydrogen) that will oxidize to form water again.

The universe of the non-social scientists is so full of closed circulating systems, equal actions and reactions, quantities that are the growth rates or decay rates of other interesting quantities, and quantities that occur in proportion to the disappearance of other quantities, that a theoretical system is often suspect until it has been grounded in a few invariances of this sort. Statisticians are trained to look for measures that are invariant under certain transformations. Logisticians who route boxcars or make up airline and school bus schedules work with semi-closed systems—some buses or planes being down for repairs, some new ones undelivered, some rental vehicles available if somebody else hasn't rented them or left them at a distant destination.

And, as I mentioned, economics is built on double-entry and quadruple-entry transactions, reciprocal flows of values in input-output matrices, quantities that are the growth rates of other quantities (as construction is to the housing stock or commercial lending is to the money supply), and quantities like gambling debts, or corporate debts and bond holdings, that are fungible and occur in offsetting positive and negative modes, or even the simple "market" in which, no matter what the capabilities and the intentions of the buyers and sellers may be, the amount bought (appropriately defined) has to equal the amount sold.

In the physical sciences, these equivalences and invariances are sometimes called laws and principles (subject of course to amendment or enlargement, as when it is discovered that heat may be converted into mechanical energy, at a fixed exchange rate, and converted back via friction at the same exchange rate). In economics and the other social sciences, they have more modest names: "market-balance equations," "accounting statements," or sometimes "social accounts." Demography is the social science that is most like economics in being built on transactions, transitions, durable quantities, events that occur in pairs, relations that are reciprocal or symmetrical, and countable or measurable things that enter the system and leave the system or change their state within the system at a small number of entries, exits, and transition points. Economics and demography deal with countable entities, many of which preserve their identities, and with measurable quantities and with activities like marriage and divorce, sale and purchase, that are discrete and well-defined, often symmetrical, sometimes reversible. In the other social sciences, there is less of a tradition for seeking out these frameworks within which populations circulate or transactions occur subject to numerical or quantitative constraints.

Lacking a logical scheme or an exhaustive classification for these several numerical and quantitative patterns and structures, the most I can do is to offer a suggestive list of some of the ways that these constraining frameworks arise.

First, a great many phenomena occur in pairs. This is often because transactions occur between two participants, sometimes because activities are two-sided or reciprocal. For every borrower there is a lender, for every tenant a landlord, for every sender a receiver; to every sale corresponds a purchase and to every payment corresponds a receipt; to a productive activity there corresponds an accrual of income, and to the burglar there corresponds a victim. Both sides of the phenomenon that occurs in pairs need not be interesting; but if they are, and if they are both well-defined and countable, and especially if they are interesting for different reasons, they will be subject not only to an equivalence relation of the kind we have been discussing, but sometimes to an unexpected one.

Second, some populations and some measurable quantities are guided by a "principle of conservation" in a closed system. Money is not destroyed by being handed from one person to another, from buyer to seller or from lender to borrower; people do not disappear when they move from city to city; heat is not lost from the larger system when it goes up the chimney; DDT does not disappear from the ecosystem when the animal that contained it is eaten by another; and waste does not always disappear when we dump it in somebody else's backyard.

Third, there are measurable quantities and countable populations that move through or within "semi-closed" systems. The simplest is merely a "turnstile" at which the waiting line equals cumulative arrivals less those who have passed through, and those who have passed equal all who arrived less those who are queued up. Slightly more complex is a succession of bottlenecks, through which everyone or everything passes in the same direction, with individuals between milestones or queued up at the turnstiles. Others include (1) the reservoir, like the elementary school through which everybody passes, or an army of inductees that some people bypass while others enter, stay at for a while, and depart; (2) alternating systems, like commuter bridges and tunnels, or circulating systems like our ski lift; (3) systems like the age profile of a population, or the rank profile of a hierarchical system, that people enter and transit in one direction only, dropping out along the way by death or retirement; (4) more complicated systems, like the criminal justice system, in which people are in jail, in court, on parole, on probation, out on bail, under observation, or repeating a transit for the second or third time, not everybody following the same route through the system, and with or without a "loop" through which some people cycle back and repeat parts of the system; and (5) free migration in which the movement is unrestricted as to direction but all takes place within a boundary that allows entry and exist in a limited number of ways. (The general format would be called a "transition matrix.")

Fourth, there are activities and relations that involve complementary population sets, of which the two sexes are an example: "singular pairing," as in monogamous marriage, and "multiple pairing," as in sibling relations; phasing relations between synchronized flows of men and women with respect to age of marriage, death, and divorce; and joint distributions among, say, the white and the non-white populations, or between people and the houses they occupy, or people and the autos they own.

Fifth, there are those variables that are separately interesting but of which one happens to be the birth rate or death rate or net rate of increase of the other. The *increment* in the population immune to some infectious disease is the number who have the disease minus the number who currently die from it, just as the number of new cars one year old or less is the gross annual increase in the number of all cars.

Sixth, the independent variable in a system of behavior often proves to be the sum of the dependent variables in the system. My decision to drive may depend on how much traffic there is; my decision how to vote may depend on whether I expect to be in the majority; my decision to stock up on a scarce good may depend on how rapidly the good is disappearing from the shelves; my decision to go to the beach, or to stay there, may depend on the density of people at the beach; and how much I contribute to the United Fund may depend on how much others contribute. But together we determine the traffic density, the population density, the coffee scarcity, the total contributions to the United Fund, or the size of the majority vote. It may or not not occur to me that I am part of your problem as you are part of mine, that my reaction to the environment is part of the environment, or that the quantity or number I am responding to is the sum of the reactions of other people reacting like me. But if we study what determines who it is that drives on a congested road, joins a burgeoning fashion, departs a declining neighborhood, or rushes to the ski resort to get there ahead of the crowds, we discover that people are reacting to a totality of which they are a part.

Seventh, and closely related, are the independent variables that prove to be the averages or other statistical consequences of the behavior that they induce. Grading students a little below or tipping waiters a little above the average, arriving a little ahead of time to be sure of a parking space or arriving a little late so as not to waste time waiting for others to arrive, or joining a tennis foursome in which one can be second best out of four, are examples.

Eighth, sometimes two different variables have a common component. Married men and women in the same population were an earlier example; in economic accounting, sales *from* firms *to* firms equal purchases by firms from firms, so that the difference between total sales and total purchases is the same as the difference between sales of goods and services to final users and payments directly to individuals, governments, and other non-firm suppliers.

Ninth, the "exhaustive subdivision" deserves to be listed. If every death has a cause imputed to it, no cause can decline in significance without the other causes together increasing.

As for the gin and the vermouth, a spoonful of gin was delivered into the vermouth vessel and a spoonful of liquid returned. We don't know how the mixture was stirred but it doesn't matter. Whatever fraction of the returned spoonful is vermouth, the rest is gin, so the gin left behind occupied the same part of a spoonful as the vermouth carried on the return trip. (In the same way, if we fill a bus with boys and take them to the girls' school, and take exactly a bus-full of children back, the seats occupied by girls on the way back must equal the seats left vacant by boys who stayed behind.)

For rowing to the bottle and back, the river is no different from a lake; the river's flow is common to bottle and boat and cancels out. We don't need to know the man's rowing speed. If he rowed away from the bottle for half an hour it took him, at the same rowing speed, a half hour to return to the bottle. With the river flowing two miles per hour, the bottle must have travelled two miles.

In the third problem you'll have to break a tile. To see this, imagine the 16 by 16 area divided like a checkerboard into 256 one-foot squares. Label the rows and columns from 1 to 16 and in each square write the sum of row and column. Adjacent squares in the same row or in the same column will have numbers that differ by one, so half of all the squares are odd and half are even and of any two adjacent squares one is odd and one is even. Every tile then covers an odd-numbered square and an even-numbered one. All the tiles together must cover as many odd as even. But the upper right (northeast) square is odd—$1 + 16 = 17$, and the southwest (lower left) square is also odd—$16 + 1 = 17$. So we should have to cover 128 even squares and only 126 odd squares, with tiles that always cover one of each. Alternatively, color the 256 one-foot squares like a checkerboard, starting with white in the upper left corner. The northeast square is black and so is the southwest square; every tile covers one white square and one black. To do the job, we should have to cover 128 white squares and 126 black squares while covering equal numbers of black and white. Or, just to close with some social science, let the 256 squares be seats in an auditorium, the left rear and right front seats to be allotted to ushers, and the sexes to alternate from left to right in every row and from front to rear in every column. Can we invite 127 married couples to the performance?

3

THERMOSTATS, LEMONS,
AND OTHER
FAMILIES OF MODELS

THE HOME THERMOSTAT is an instructive device. It is the intelligence of the heating system. It controls the temperature by responding to the temperature. The system including the thermostat is a *model* of many behavior systems—human, vegetable, and mechanical. It is a "model" because it reproduces the essential features of those other behaviors in a transparent way.

The furnace heats water. Heating water takes time. The water circulates in radiators that heat the air. Heating air takes time. Rising temperature at the thermostat expands a piece of metal that breaks electrical contact, turning the furnace off; falling temperature contracts the metal and reverses the switch to the furnace. Outdoor temperature, wind, and insulation determine the heat loss from the building and, hence, the speed with which warm radiators can influence that metal contact by inducing a flow of warm air.

If the system is up to the task of attaining the desired temperature, it generates a cyclical process. The temperature rises in the morning to the level for which the thermostat is set—and overshoots it. It always does. The temperature then falls back to the setting—and undershoots it. It rises again and overshoots it. The house never just warms up to the desired temperature and remains there.

At the first peak (overshoot) temperature in the morning, somebody may be tempted to lower the thermostat setting. Lowering it has two effects: it makes the temperature go farther below the desired temperature than it was going to go anyhow; and, paradoxically, when the thermostat is reset after the house gets cold, the next peak will be higher above the desired setting than it would have been if nobody had fooled with the thing!

The thermostat is smart but not very smart. For more

money you can get a smarter one that acts as though it thinks ahead. If you set it for 70 and the temperature is below 68 it turns the furnace off at 68, but if the temperature is above 72 the furnace will go on at 72. It responds not only to temperature but to the direction the temperature is going.

What the system is a model of is various cyclical processes. These are processes that generate alternating ups and downs. They contain mechanisms that cause a rising variable to overshoot and then turn down and undershoot. What it overshoots and undershoots is some level that, in its own fashion, it is "seeking."

The thermostat system is so simple that we can see why the overshoot occurs. The furnace has only two states, on and off. When it is on it is on full blast. It stays on until the air temperature reaches the setting of the thermostat. While the furnace is on, the water in the radiators gets hotter and hotter; when the furnace goes off, the radiators are at peak temperature. No wonder the house goes on getting hotter. But as the house gets hotter the radiators get cooler, until they are no longer able to raise the air temperature. The temperature is above the thermostat setting; the furnace is off; and the radiators continue to cool as the house cools until the temperature is back to the thermostat setting. The thermostat then turns the furnace back on but the house continues to cool until the water in the radiators has been reheated. This is where we came in. The process repeats. If the system is "well behaved" the ups and downs will become smaller and eventually settle on a steady wave motion whose amplitude depends on the time lags in the system.

And it is the time lags that generate the cycles. If the furnace were an open hearth with no radiators, the house would cool immediately once the desired temperature were reached, and the furnace would alternate like a buzzer, keeping the temperature even.

The more expensive thermostat coupled to the hot water system thinks ahead in a purely mechanical way. With rising temperature it turns off at 68 rather than 70; it overshoots to 73 instead of 76; on the return it switches on at 72 and the radiators are warm again about the time the temperature crosses 70. This time there is little undershoot.

In addition, at more expense than home heating systems will usually justify, the furnace can have two settings: low and high. It will operate at full blast when room temperaature is many degrees below the setting and switch to low as the room approaches 70. This, too, will damp but not altogether eliminate the temperature cycles.

Consider, now, the passengers on a cruise ship as they congregate along the starboard rail on the top deck to watch a school of porpoises. The ship is dangerously overloaded and begins to list badly to starboard. As the starboard rail seems to sink, the passengers scramble up the sloping deck to get farther from danger, possibly thinking that by doing so they will help the ship right itself. A few of them reach the port rail and the ship recovers somewhat; with the reduced slope, more passengers can make it up the deck. Eventually, the ship nearly level, they all make it across the center line, watching with relief as the ship continues to right itself and the deck becomes more nearly level. Their relief does not last; for, at the instant the ship is level, there are two things working against stability. First, the passengers are all on the side toward which it is tipping. Second, its rolling momentum would carry it well over to port even if the passengers could instantaneously distribute themselves in a balanced way over the deck. The scene witnessed by the porpoises on the starboard side a minute ago will now be seen by the children in their sailboats on the port side, as the passengers scramble back up toward the "safety" of the starboard side.

A friend of mine once managed a measle-vaccine program for infants in a poor country. At the outset the program was successful; the disease had been serious, and mothers brought their infants long distances to be vaccinated. Shortly, most infants were vaccinated, and the unvaccinated were too few to sustain an epidemic. For more than a year there was no measles. By then there was a new population of unvaccinated infants, large enough to sustain an epidemic. The epidemic killed some children, immunized others, and scared mothers, who then brought their infants long distances to be vaccinated. It was another year before the disease was forgotten and the mothers stopped coming, and still another year before the new unvaccinated population invited the next epidemic.

In this measles cycle the upswing and the downswing are generated differently. The downswing relates to the response time of mothers in the aftermath of an epidemic; the upswing is generated by the epidemiological response time of measles to a new population. One might be measured in months and the other in years, with a pattern less like wave motion than like a succession of independent surges. It remains to be seen whether polio in a rich country, or even smallpox (unless it is at last truly extinct), may repeat that pattern of measles in a poor country.

The phenomenon of overshoot is a familiar one at the level of the individual. A child can eat chocolate, or his parent drink alcohol, until he feels that he has had enough. When he feels that he has had enough he has usually had too much. The alcohol in the stomach is like hot water in radiators: it is already in the system but hasn't yet been noticed by the thermostat. Five minutes after he stops eating the chocolate the child can still taste it, and it no longer tastes so good.

Numerous social phenomena display cyclical behavior, either in wave motion or in surges. The thermostat reminds us to look for the time lag, or for an accumulated inventory like the hot water. At the time of Sputnik there was alarm about a shortage of scientists and engineers in America, and a multitude of programs were funded to produce more scientists and engineers. The process is slow because it takes time to recruit youngsters into science and engineering and to graduate them with college training and advanced degrees. The "pipeline" begins somewhere in high school and has its outlet half a

dozen years later in a young person's career. Unless the system
has one of those expensive thermostats that shuts off the program and reduces the pipeline to normal several years before
the perceived shortage has disappeared, the *production* (not
the number) of new scientists and engineers is likely to be at a
peak just when the thermostat says, "That's it." Like the hot
water in the radiators, there is a six-year's supply of scientists
and engineers coming along in the system; and we might guess
that the surplus will build up for six years leaving an "over-
hang" that will depress and discourage recruitment for most of
a generation. When the supply at last gets back to normal,
some years hence, replenishment will be at an abnormally low
level, with a "famine" that will get worse for at least six years
before it can begin to get better. And then the cycle can start
over.

Models in the Social Sciences

Cyclical behavior is one of those kinds of social behavior
for which it can be helpful to have a set of familiar models. By
"model" I mean either of two things. A model can be a precise
and economical statement of a set of relationships that are sufficient to produce the phenomenon in question. Or, a model
can be an actual biological, mechanical, or social system that
embodies the relationships in an especially transparent way,
producing the phenomenon as an obvious consequence of
those relationships. These two meanings of "model" are not
very different; what makes the heating system a useful model
is that we can describe it so precisely and so tersely that we
can convert it almost directly to mathematical form. Each of us
in thinking about that system may have in mind some particular house, radiators and all; but the shape and location of the
house, the room and window arrangements, the fuel in the furnace, and the climate in which the actual house is located
don't really intrude. We can agree on the model without sharing images of the houses we have in mind.

The furnace is merely an object that has two states, on and off. The temperature of the water is a variable that approaches room temperature when the furnace is off and rises when the furnace is on. Room temperature is a variable that approaches the outdoor temperature when the water temperature is low and rises toward some upper limit, depending on outside temperature, when the water temperature is high. The thermostat itself is simply a rule of behavior, stating that the furnace is "on" when room temperature is below a specified level, "off" above that level.

We can enlarge the "model" by admitting outdoor temperature as another variable; we then relate the critical level of water temperature to the outdoor temperature, using the principle that heat loss from the building is proportionate to the difference between indoor and outdoor temperature, and heat loss from the radiators is proportionate to the difference between water temperature and room temperature. And if we do all this with noncommittal algebraic abbreviations, like x, y, and z rather than "water temp," "air temp," and "furnace on" or "furnace off," we have an abstract mathematical system. That is, we have a mathematical statement of exactly those characteristics of our heating system, and only those characteristics, that we want in our model—the characteristics that account for the cyclical behavior we want to study.

Furthermore, *we have a mathematical description that is now independent of the heating system.* Any variable x that increases or decreases according to the level of another variable, y, which increases or decreases according to whether still another variable, z, has a value of "on" or "off" (where the latter is on or off according to whether the value of x is above or below some target level), will behave like our heating system. The heating system is one "representation" of this system of relationships. Anything else we can find that is *described* by the model will *behave* as the model behaves.

Whether or not that is any help depends, of course, on whether we can find other things that are both interesting and described by the model, and on whether we need the model—whether the model gives us a head start in recognizing phenomena and the mechanisms that generate them and in knowing what to look for in the explanation of interesting phenomena. If the model is very simple, it may explain only very simple events, and for events so simple we may not need any model. If the model is complicated, it may be too specialized to fit any events except the particular events from which we derived it; in that case, it can be useful only as a compact formula for the particular phenomenon we have already analyzed. Models tend to be useful when they are simultaneously simple enough to fit a variety of behaviors and complex enough to fit behaviors that need the help of an explanatory model.

If a model meets the criterion of simplicity it will often, like the thermostat-controlled heating system, describe physical and mechanical systems as well as social phenomena, animal behavior as well as human, scientific principles as well as household activities. An example is "critical mass." An atomic pile "goes critical" when a chain reaction of nuclear fission becomes self-sustaining; for an atomic pile, or an atomic bomb, there is some minimum amount of fissionable material that has to be compacted together to keep the reaction from petering out. But boy scouts have known for half a century, and all mankind knew before them, that wood fire displays the same phenomenon: try to get a single stick of firewood to burn by itself. The principle of critical mass is so simple that it is no wonder that it shows up in epidemiology, fashion, survival and extinction of species, language systems, racial integration, jaywalking, panic behavior, and political movements.

Most of the models used in the social sciences are families rather than individual models. There is no single model of cyclical behavior, or any unique model of "critical mass," but rather a family of related models that differ in some characteristics but share some essential features. Measles vaccination shares some crucial features with the thermostat system but differs in important respects. A measles-epidemic model without vaccination will be different but recognizable as a member of the family. And models that portray cyclical fashions in clothing or in the first names of children, the cyclical interaction of parasite and host populations, or economic cycles in the shipbuilding industry will differ while being significantly alike.

The same will be true of critical-mass phenomena. A model is a tool; to be useful, it has to be adjustable or to consist of a set from which we can select the appropriate member. The wrench is a tool of universal application, but a single rigid wrench that fits only hexagonal three-quarter-inch nuts won't open many secrets for us.

This chapter is about some of the families of models that are widely used in the social sciences. Many of them have counterparts in animal ecology, epidemiology, or the physical sciences. They are not whole theories, just models of recurrent behavior patterns that are best recognized and compared with each other by the help of familiar models. A shared model is help in communicating, especially if the model has a name.

There is not, as far as I am aware, any standard collection of these familiar models. Some of the models are most familiar to economists, others to sociologists, some to epidemiologists, some to traffic engineers. Some are used by students of racial segregation who may not know that similar models are used in the study of animal ecology; some are used in economics while similar models may be used in demography. It enhances one's appreciation of a model, and often the use one can make of it, to be aware of applications outside one's own field. Recognition of the wide applicability of a model, or of a family of models, helps in recognizing that one is dealing with a very general or basic phenomenon, not something specialized or idiosyncratic or unique.

The chapter is not intended as a definitive list of the families of models most widely used. The purpose is to illustrate that there are such families of models that cut across different fields of inquiry and different problem areas, to suggest that such families of models are not only valuable tools but more valuable, the more familiar one is with the diversity of phenomena to which they apply, and to suggest that the student of social sciences should be alert to the occurrence of such models and should add new families of models to his repertoire whenever he can find them.

Models often overlap. The measles epidemic is usually a critical-mass process.[4] A succession of epidemics, with intervening periods in which the pool of susceptibles renews itself, corresponds to a cyclical model. And the acceleration principle mentioned in Chapter 2 can also be discerned in the epidemic: the current infection rate—the number actually sick with measles—is the diminution rate of the susceptibles and, with the mortality rate subtracted, the rate of increase in the immune population.

A "bounded-neighborhood model" will be used in Chapter 4 to study the mixing and separating of races, or of any two populations that can migrate in or out of some neighborhood. The same analytic scheme, with a different interpretation, serves also for two species that increase or decrease. Biologists use the same kind of model for studying the growth and decline, survival and extinction, of competing species, reciprocally beneficial species, and predators and their prey. Kenneth Boulding has used such ecological models to study group conflict.[5]

Critical Mass, Tipping, and Lemons

A common occurrence among the Harvard faculty is the "dying seminar." Somebody organizes a group of twenty-five who are eager to meet regularly to pursue a subject of common interest. It meets at some hour at which people

[4] A rudimentary model to study measles epidemics, and a comparison of the results with data for different cities, is lucidly presented by Maurice S. Bartlett in "Epidemics," in *Statistics: A Guide to the Unknown*, eds. Judith M. Tanur and Frederick Mosteller (Holden-Day, Inc., 1972), pp. 66–76.

[5] J. Maynard Smith, *Models in Ecology* (Cambridge University Press, 1974), especially Chapter 5, "Competition," and Kenneth E. Boulding, *Conflict and Defense* (Harper and Brothers, 1962), Chapter 6, "The Group as a Party to Conflict: The Ecological Model."

expect to be free. The first meeting has a good turnout, three-quarters or more, a few having some conflict. By the third or fourth meeting the attendance is not much more than half and pretty soon only a handful attend. Eventually the enterprise lapses, by consent among the few at a meeting or by the organizers' giving up and arranging no more.

The original members then express regret that it didn't work. Everybody is sorry that the others didn't find it worthwhile. The conclusion is drawn that the interest just wasn't there.

But it often looks as though the interest was there. The thing petered out in spite of interest. Nearly everybody, if asked, alleges that he'd have continued attending pretty regularly if enough others had cared enough to attend regularly enough to make it worthwhile.

Behind my building is a grassy area where a related social phenomenon—I think it is related—can be observed every autumn, as if it were an experiment. Somebody puts up the volleyball net, gathers a few friends, starts a game, and attracts a few more players. Then one of two things happens. By the second or third day, a pretty good crowd has gathered to play volleyball; people begin to get acquainted; there's discussion of what the best time to play is; there are bystanders willing to join the game; the enterprise is a success and may last until the snow comes. Or, it goes the way of the dying seminar—fun but not enough fun, because there are not enough people to generate the loyalty and enthusiasm that would keep the number large and the absentee rate small.

In a single day, I can encounter half a dozen occurrences that remind me of that volleyball game. At the busiest intersection in Cambridge, a few nimble pedestrians cross against the light and cars keep coming; more pedestrians hesitate, ready to join any surge of people into the street but not willing to venture ahead without safety in numbers. People look left and right—not to watch the traffic but to watch the other pedestrians! At some point several appear to decide that the flow of pedestrians is large enough to be safe and they join it, enlarg-

ing it further and making it safe for a few who were still waiting and who now join. Soon, even the timid join what has
become a crowd. The drivers see they no longer have any
choice and stop. At less busy intersections, smaller bands of
pedestrians hesitate as a few of the adventurous step into the
traffic, looking anxiously back to see who's following; too few
to intimidate the traffic, and unable to get the troops out of the
trenches behind them, the leaders fall back to the curb.

On the last day of class a few students, acting out of duty,
politeness, or appreciation, begin to applaud hesitantly as the
instructor gathers his materials to leave the room. If enough
clap, the whole class may break into applause; if a few clap
indecisively, it dwindles to an embarrassed silence. On all days
except the last day of class, the instructor who keeps talking
after the end of the hour notices that students, like the pedestrians at the curb, lean toward the door, shuffle, put books
away, occasionally stand up, hoping to start enough of an
exodus to keep any departing students from being conspicuous.

I walk across the lawn if that seems to be what others are
doing; I sometimes double-park if it looks as though everybody is double-parked. I stay in line if everybody is standing
politely in line, but if people begin to surge toward the ticket
window I am alert to be—though never among the first—not
among the last. If a few people get away with smoking in a
no-smoking section, perhaps because the people who should
tell them not to are momentarily preoccupied, so many others
light up that the cause becomes hopeless and they are not even
told to stop, or, if told, don't. Meanwhile, the newspapers
report that certain old residential areas are deteriorating; they
are deteriorating because the people who keep their homes
attractive are leaving; they are leaving because the neighborhood is deteriorating because people like them are leaving
because the neighborhood is deteriorating. . . . In some
schools, the white pupils are being withdrawn because there
are too few white pupils; as they leave, white pupils become

fewer so that even those who didn't mind yesterday's ratio will leave at today's ratio, leaving behind still fewer, who may leave tomorrow. At other schools, black students, with what is reported to be the same motivation, are leaving because they find themselves too few for safety and comfort, and as they leave they aggravate the fewness for those they leave behind.

What is common to all of these examples is the way people's behavior depends on *how many* are behaving a particular way, or how much they are behaving that way—how many attend the seminar how frequently, how many play volleyball how frequently; how many smoke, or double-park; how many applaud and how loudly; how many leave the dying neighborhood and how many leave the school.

The generic name for behaviors of this sort is *critical mass*. Social scientists have adopted the term from nuclear engineering, where it is common currency in connection with atomic bombs. If radioactive decay occurs in a substance like uranium, neutrons are emitted that fly into space unless they hit other nuclei before they leave the mass of uranium, in which case they produce a couple of new neutrons that do the same thing. If the amount of uranium is small, each neutron traverses a small volume containing other atoms and, since most of the volume is "empty space" from a neutron's point of view, there is only a small amount of induced additional activity. If the amount of uranium is large, there is a greater likelihood that a neutron will produce two more neutrons rather than fly unobstructed into space. If there is enough uranium so that half the neutrons produce two others, the process is self-sustaining and a "critical mass" of uranium is said to be present. Any larger amount of uranium will lead each neutron to produce on the average more than one neutron: an explosive chain reaction occurs (as when each grain of gunpowder ignites other grains in an enclosed space) that could consume all the uranium (except that the mass of uranium may fl apart and halt the activity).

If we stick very close to the bomb analogy and deal only

with a "mass" of people, about the only example I can think of is body warmth. One person standing alone radiates heat into space, two people reflect each other's heat, a roomful of people can keep each other warm, and if you pack enough people together, even in cold weather, they will overheat themselves.

But even with the atomic bomb, "mass" is not strictly correct. The density, purity, and shape of the uranium, as well as its mass, together with any reflective coating, will determine whether or not the lump "goes critical." Furthermore, mass is proportionate to the number of atoms, and *critical number* could have been equally apt.

For our purpose we can think of critical mass as shorthand for critical number, critical density, critical ratio, or in special cases like body heat and the production of carbon dioxide, actual mass. What all of the critical-mass models involve is some activity that is self-sustaining once the measure of that activity passes a certain minimum level. But whether the measure is the number of people engaged, or the number times the frequency or the length of time they engage in it, or the ratio of the number who do to the number who do not, or the amount of such activity per square foot or per day or per telephone extension, we can call it a "critical-mass" activity and a lot of people will know what we mean. By "activity" I specifically mean to include just being (or not being) someplace: if everybody will stay if enough others do, and the total number is more than "enough," everybody will stay; and everybody will go if not enough are present. Ratios rather than numbers may be involved if it is blacks and whites or men and women or English-speaking and French-speaking residing in a neighborhood or enrolling in a school or staying with some social event or political activity.

The variety of critical-mass models is great. In one version, people make their decision on the basis of actual numbers—being attracted to the majority party, volunteering on condition that twenty others do likewise, staying at a meeting if attendance is sufficient, or voting "guilty" on a jury's verdict.

In some cases, it is not the number itself but some effect of the number that matters—it is the immunity in numbers that causes people to double park if everybody else is doing it, the noise level that causes people to raise their voices to be heard, or the grudging accommodation of automobile drivers that may make bicycling safer if enough people bicycle. And for some purposes, like those neutrons in the chain reaction, the activity may involve contact between individuals—if people pass along the rumors they've heard lately, the relevant population has to be large enough for somebody to meet somebody to tell it to pretty soon or the rumor, like an infectious disease, will die away rather than spread contagiously.

Again, some of the activities are continuous and reversible —you can walk home every evening after dark if enough other people do, and quit if it appears that not enough others are out walking. Some, like getting tattooed or committing suicide, are quite irreversible. Some are a single occurrence; you prefer to wear blue jeans to an official meeting unless most of the people are going to be more formally dressed. Some of the choices are binary—whether to pass on the right or the left; some are among multiple alternatives—which language to learn, to communicate with as many foreigners as possible. Sometimes the choice is on-off—whether or not to wear a tie; sometimes it is rate or intensity or frequency, as in deciding how loud to play your radio at the beach to drown out the other radios.

Though perhaps not in physical and chemical reactions, in social reactions it is typically the case that the "critical number" for one person differs from another's. You may dress formally if enough people do to keep you from being conspicuous, but I dress formally only if so many do that I would be conspicuous not to. You may be willing to enroll in a school in which the opposite sex outnumbers you no more than 3 or 4 to 1, but I may be unwilling to enroll in a school unless it is largely my own sex. You may work to support a candidate if there's any significant chance that she could win, somebody else only if her chances are better than anybody else's, and I only if I'm nearly certain that she is going to win.

The generic model therefore includes the case in which we all have the same critical point, as well as the case in which there are five of us who will show regularly for the seminar if as many as ten do; another five, for a total of ten, who will keep coming if fifteen do; thirty altogether for whom thirty is an adequate number; and fifty for whom forty is enough.

When people differ with respect to their cross-over points, there may be a large range of numbers over which, if that number of people were doing it, for a few but only a few among them that number wouldn't be big enough, while the rest would be content. When those few for whom the number is not enough drop out, they lower the number, and some more drop out, and so on all the way. The fact that in the end nobody is doing it does not give us any measure of *how many* satisfied participants were lacking at any point along the way.

In our dying seminar it could be that for any number present, two or three find it not large enough; when they drop out, another two or three find it not large enough and when they drop out, another two or three. The number along the way who, if they could be enticed or coerced into staying, would make the whole thing viable, may be small or large; the fact that it dies out completely does not tell us how near to being viable it was.

The model applies perfectly well to a situation in which some fraction of the population will engage in the activity independently of how many do, and some other fraction will not, independently of how many do. Consider the case of pass-fail grading in a law school. If the option of taking the course pass-fail (without a letter grade) is available to all students, it is usually observed that there are some who will elect pass-fail no matter how many others do, some who will elect letter grades no matter how many elect pass-fail, and an intermediate group who will elect pass-fail if enough do but will choose letter grades if pass-fail is uncommon. Notice that the first and second groups' behavior is independent of how the third group chooses, but not vice versa; the people whose behavior is uninfluenced nevertheless influence others. So we cannot just leave out of our analysis the two groups whose behavior is independently determined, and analyze only that group that displays the critical-mass phenomenon. If the two groups whose behavior is unconditional are small, there may be two sustainable outcomes: if all whose behavior is conditional are choosing pass-fail, the number (including the unconditional pass-fail choosers) is self-sustaining; and if the number choosing letter grades includes all those whose behavior is conditional, their letter-grade choice will be self-sustaining.

But there is another possibility. The unconditional–pass-fail students may be sufficient in numbers to induce some of the conditional choosers to elect pass-fail, who in turn are enough to induce some more, who in turn are enough to induce some more, and so on until all but the unconditional letter graders are electing pass-fail. In that case, there are not two self-sustaining outcomes—one with nearly everybody choosing pass-fail and the other with nearly everybody choosing letter grades —but a single ineluctable outcome. Critical mass is provided by the people whose behavior does not depend on numbers, and the chain reaction takes care of the rest.

Notice that the model itself does not tell us which outcome is preferable. There are at least three possibilities. First—and to clarify the point, let's suppose everybody's choice depends on how many choose pass-fail—it may be that everybody actually prefers pass-fail but feels uneasy about it unless enough others also choose it. Second, everybody may prefer letter grades but feel uneasy about it if most people choose pass-fail. Third, some may prefer pass-fail but feel insecure unless enough others choose it, while others prefer letter grades but feel uneasy unless enough others choose letter grades. The observed outcome may be one that everybody prefers, it may be one that nobody prefers, or it may be one that some prefer and others deplore.

So there may or may not be a unanimously preferred outcome. And even if one of the outcomes is unanimously chosen, we cannot infer that it is preferred from the fact that it is universally chosen. If everybody is on daylight saving or the metric system, or if everybody addresses women as Ms. or teachers by their first names, or everybody waits for the green light to cross at the intersection, I'll go along; if everybody feels the way I do, we'll all go along. But unless we smile or frown an observer cannot tell whether we go along joyfully or reluctantly. And, unless some of us smile and some of us frown, it may not be evident that some of us like it and some of us do not and that whichever is the custom we go along with it.

Two special terms have begun to come into currency to distinguish subclasses of critical-mass phenomena. One is *tipping*, and the other is *lemons*.

The lemons model is not only about a special kind of interdependent behavior, but has a name that illustrates it. The name is not an ancient idea or institution, like the commons, that has been newly appropriated for dramatic effect; it is not borrowed from nuclear physics or ecology or even horticulture. Nor did it just emerge through a consensual process of obscure origin. The name was picked by an economist because the "market for lemons" has interesting properties that can give insight into a variety of situations. And the lemons he had in mind are not the ones from which lemonade is made, but the kind that people drive.[6]

He argued that the seller of a used car knows whether or not it is a lemon; the buyer has to play the averages, knowing only that some cars are lemons but not whether the particular car he's buying is. Buyers will pay only a price that reflects the average frequency of lemons in the used-car crop. That average is a high price for a lemon but understates the worth of the better cars offered on the market. The owners of the better cars are reluctant to sell at a price that makes allowance for

6 Akerlof, George A., "The Market for 'Lemons': Quality Uncertainty and the Market Mechanism," *The Quarterly Journal of Economics*, 84 (August 1970), No. 3.

the lemons that other people are selling; so the better cars appear less frequently on the market and the average frequency of lemons increases. As customers learn this, they make a greater allowance for lemons in the price they're willing to pay. The cars of average quality in the previous market are now undervalued and their owners less willing to sell them. The percentage frequency of lemons continues to rise. In the end, the market may disappear, although institutional arrangements like guarantees, or the certification of cars by dealers who exploit a reputation for good cars, may keep the used-car market alive.

Akerlof generalized this model to a number of markets in which there is unequal information on the two sides—insurance companies know less than you do, usually, about whether you are accident prone, or susceptible to hereditary diseases, or are contemplating suicide. Life insurance rates for sixty-five-year-olds must allow for a large fraction who are not long for this world. And those who know they are healthy and have a family history of longevity and are exposed to few risks have to pay the same premium as the poorer risks; life insurance being unattractive at that price, few of them buy it. The average life expectancy of the customers goes down, the rates go up further, and the bargain now looks poor even to those of normal life expectancy. And so forth.

This process will show up in Chapter 5 in the recruitment of "young" elderly people to an older persons' home. It is akin to, and sometimes coincides with, those situations in which the below average, or the above average, withdraw or won't join, causing some potential market or institution to unravel. Because people vary and because averages matter, there may be no sustainable critical mass; and the unravelling behavior, or initial failure to get the activity going at all, has much the appearance of a critical mass that is almost but not quite achieved. This is therefore a kindred but separate family of models.

I said that Akerlof's lemons model has a name that illustrates critical mass. "Lemons" appears to be over the hump and on its way to permanence in the language but in case it is not, maybe my readers can give it the boost it needs.

Tipping is a name that was first applied to neighborhood migration. It was observed that the entrance of a few members of a minority into a neighborhood often caused some among the formerly homogeneous population to leave, or to show signs of leaving. Their departure left openings, so more members of the minority could enter; the increase in new residents induced more of the old to leave, and so forth in the familiar process. Some of the departures might be motivated by the minority entrants who had already arrived, some by the belief that the process, once started, would continue, and some by the fear that they might soon be selling their houses in panic. Among early writers on the subject, the model was not explicit. The concept came to be applied to schools and school districts in the 1960s, racial minorities again being the stimulus and white-pupil-departure the phenomenon. The concept came to be applied to occupations, clubs and fraternities, medical schools and colleges, public beaches and tennis courts, restaurants, nightclubs and public parks.

It also became apparent that there was a complementary process of "tipping-in" as well as one of "tipping-out." Not only was the departure of a white population induced by the appearance of minorities, but minorities themselves would be more attracted the larger the minority colony and the faster its growth, with some minimum size required to get a self-sustaining influx started. For tipping-in as well as for tipping-out, part of the process may involve expectations—people do not wait until the alien colony exceeds their toleration before departing, nor do the minority entrants wait until comfortable numbers have been achieved, as long as they can foresee the numbers increasing with any confidence.

The tipping model is a special case—a broad class of special cases—of critical-mass phenomena. Its characteristics are usually that people have very different cross-over points; that the behavior involves place of residence or work or recreation or, in general, *being* someplace rather than *doing* something; that the critical numbers relate to two or more distinct groups, and each group may be separately tipping out or tipping in; and that the process involves conscious decisions and anticipations. It may be on a scale as small as the dining hall table that is abandoned by whites when blacks begin to sit there or as large as the white population of Rhodesia.

Diagrammatics of Critical Mass

Critical-mass models can be illuminated with a family of diagrams, a few of which will be illustrated here. To generate such a diagram we suppose that for some activity—attending, say, the optional Saturday morning review session that goes with a lecture course—there are some people who will attend regularly no matter what the attendance is and some who will never attend, but most people will attend if, but only if, enough others do. Everybody has his own definition of how many is "enough." And it can mean either enough to make it interesting or enough to make it imprudent to be absent.

For everybody whose attendance depends on the attendance he anticipates, we have a number: the minimum attendance that will just induce this person to attend. It could be absolute or a percentage of the total; if the class consists of 100 we can think of numbers or percentages. The people for whom we have such numbers are fewer than 100 if there are some whose decisions are immune to the attendance of others. We tabulate the people for whom the critical number is 50 or 20 or 1 or 75 and construct a bar chart, the height of the bar indicating for how many people the critical number is between 20 and 25, 25 and 30, and so forth. We idealize the bar chart into a smooth frequency distribution. It will have the familiar shape of an inverted bell if the critical numbers cluster around some average value and taper off in both directions; it could be two-humped or U-shaped if the population consists of distinct groups whose averages cluster around different values or pile up at the ends of the scale. This frequency distribution, together with the number who unconditionally attend, generates our diagram.

The diagram is nothing but this frequency distribution converted to *cumulative* form. The cumulative form measures, for any number of anticipated attendance, the number of people for whom that number is large enough. It is "cumulative" because it includes, at any point along the horizontal scale, all the people who are located to the left of that point in the original distribution. At 35 it registers all the people whose critical numbers are no larger than 35; at 45 it includes them plus those whose numbers are between 35 and 45. At 100 it indicates all who will show up if everybody is expected. This cumulative curve rises steadily to the right, or at least never declines, because the number preferring to attend is assumed to be larger, the larger the anticipated attendance. (If there were some who would attend only if the number were not too large, preferring intimacy rather than crowds, we would need two distributions, one for the number of people for whom a particular attendance was just enough, the other the number for whom it is just too much, and the cumulative curve would be the cumulative difference between them. It could then decline as well as rise from left to right.)

This cumulative curve begins on the vertical axis at a height denoting those who would attend even if nobody else did, rises to the right over the range from zero to 100, picking up all the people whose attendance depends on anticipated attendance, and at 100 on the horizontal axis records everybody except those who never attend.

The *steepness* of this cumulative curve is proportionate to the *height* of the frequency distribution. If the original distribution is bell-shaped, the cumulative curve will increase in steepness to the point where the original distribution is at its maximum, diminish in steepness thereafter, with what is leniently called an S-shape.

Such a curve is Figure 1. According to this curve nobody will attend unless a few are expected, 85 will attend if everybody is expected, and for most people the critical number is between a third and half the total. (The frequency distribution that underlies this curve, whose height is proportionate to the steepness of this curve, is sharply peaked at 45 percent of the total, nearly but not quite symmetrical, and contains 85 percent of the population; the majority are bunched from 35 to 55). The 45-degree dashed line is for reference. Its height is always equal to its rightward distance, and it tells at a glance whether the people for whom a particular number is enough are more or less than that number. We quickly see that there are not 25 people for whom 25 is enough, the curve being

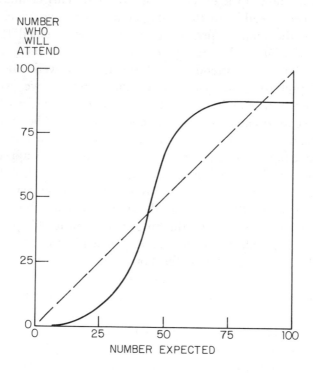

Figure 1

below the 45 degree line at 25, but more than 60 for whom 60 is enough.

Suppose 25 or 30 people were expected to attend, possibly because that's the number who attended last week. With that expectation there are only a dozen who will show up, and most of them will be disappointed, only one or two wanting to attend with a dozen. Next week we should expect almost nobody, and nobody at all the week after. If instead two-thirds are expected, three-quarters will show up, none disappointed, and there are still others who would have appeared had these 75 been expected. And next week if 75 are expected 80 or more will show, and by the following week all will be present who would ever attend. If more than 85 are expected 85 will attend, none disappointed, and the 85 should continue.

What we have is two stable equilibria. One is with 85 expected and 85 attending, the other is with none expected and none attending. Any number less than 40 will contain some who are disappointed and drop out, lowering attendance so that others drop out, successively until nobody's left. Any number in excess of 40 not only can be satisfied but will attract more, who raise the number and attract still more, until all 85 are attending. If exactly 40 are expected 40 will attend, but any small divergence upward or downward will attract a few more or repel a few, and the number will grow to 85 or decline to zero. Attendance of 40 is an unstable equilibrium.

Three other possibilities are shown in Figure 2. Curve C shows a dozen people who will attend independently of the number: the curve begins at 12 on the verticle axis. The attendance of those 12 will draw another few, and there is a stable equilibrium at 16 or 18. If the number expected is 25 or 30, fewer than 25 or 30 will attend and people will drop out until only those 16 or 18 are attending. We have an unstable equilibrium near 50 percent and the other stable equilibrium again at 85.

Curve A reflects our dying seminar; critical mass cannot be achieved. About a quarter of the people will attend if half do,

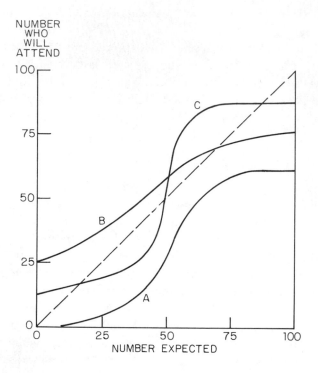

Figure 2

half will attend if two-thirds do, and two-thirds will attend if everybody does. But not everybody will. There is no self-sustaining level of attendance.

In Curve *B* critical mass is no problem. Any expectation from zero up to 70 will attract that number and more, the number converging on the single stable equilibrium where the curve crosses the 45 degree line. An expectation greater than 70 will not be sustained and the process will converge on 70.

Curve *B* is representative of a family of models, cousins to critical mass, that have interesting "multiplier effects." With any curve like *B* we can ask what happens to the equilibrium number when we remove a few who always attend or induce a few to attend who never attended before. Specifically, what happens if, among those 25 who according to Curve *B* attend unconditionally, a dozen become unable to attend? Their inability to attend lowers the curve parallel to itself, 12 units down the vertical scale. (Renumbering the vertical scale, replacing 12 with zero, and shifting the 45-degree line up 12 units, does the trick.) The equilibrium now occurs at 25. Forty-five fewer people are attending, 33 of them because of the smaller attendance. The ratio, 45/12 or 3.75, is the "multiplier effect."

The formula for the multiplier depends on the steepness of the curve. The steepness is not uniform, but the average slope between the old and the new equilibrium is evidently $(45-12) \div 45$, or $1-(12/45)$. If S is the slope and M is the multiplier, S equals $1-(1/M)$, and $M = 1/(1-S)$. If the slope were ½ the multiplier would be 2; slopes of ¼ and ¾ generate multipliers of 4/3 and 4. (The slope cannot exceed 1 and cross the 45 degree line from above as *B* does.)

Not shown is a curve representing "congestion": the greater the number anticipated, the fewer will wish to attend. Such a curve would begin high on the vertical axis at the left, indicating the people who would attend if they could have the place to themselves, and slope down to the right showing smaller numbers attending, the larger the expected attendance. Evidently it will cross the 45-degree line exactly once, offering a single stable equilibrium.

A special case, just for practice, might be a local skating rink that attracts two kinds of skaters: a few professional skaters who prefer empty ice and lots of recreational skaters who don't like it either crowded or lonely. The small serious group is represented by a downward sloping curve that crosses the 45-degree line toward the lower left. The larger sociable group shows a hill-shaped cumulative curve beginning somewhere out along the horizontal axis, swooping up well above the 45-degree line, and turning downward beyond a point where larger numbers are less attractive. Combining the two populations, we add the numbers from both groups that wish to attend for any given level of attendance, obtaining a curve that starts a small way up the axis, slopes downward, and may or may not reach the 45-degree line before swooping upward, eventually crossing the 45-degree line well to the upper right.

If there is only that one intersection, the downward slope to the lower left curving upward before the 45-degree line is reached, the serious skaters will not skate at all. Their numbers are enough to attract some sociable skaters, who attract more until their numbers make the place unattractive to the serious skaters. (The picture is a little like our curve labelled B if at the lower left it had a U-shaped portion starting at the vertical axis.) Notice that if there are no serious skaters there is an equilibrium at zero occupancy, not enough sociable skaters wishing to attend at low attendance. Thus the presence of the serious skaters generates enough attendance to attract the sociable skaters, who crowd out the serious.

Alternatively, if numbers and preferences are such that an equilibrium of serious skaters is reached at levels well below what attracts the sociable skaters, the curve initially dipping below the 45-degree line before curving upward to cross it again, there are two equilibria. One is a crowd of friendly skaters, with far too much congestion to attract the serious; the other is a modest number of serious skaters, the rink too lonely for most of the population. Of course, if the sociable skaters "mistakenly" expect a large attendance and show up accordingly, they will confirm their own expectations and attract still more the next day.

In the attendance example we had a fixed population of students, but for different population sizes is it percentages or absolute numbers that matter? Undoubtedly for some behaviors, like language and fashion and perhaps those Saturday sections, it is proportions that influence people, not absolute numbers, while for other behaviors—playing chess, participating in a play-reading group, or possibly attending that Saturday section—it will be absolute numbers that attract or repel. So we should expect both. And it makes a difference.

One difference is that if absolute numbers are what matter, and if the influence is positive so that the more who do it the more will wish to, the activity is likely to be self-sustaining in a large group but not in a small one.

If it is proportions that matter—smoking cigarettes or wearing turtlenecks or speaking with a particular accent depending on the fraction of the relevant population that does so—there is the possibility of dividing or separating populations. If people are influenced by local populations—the people they live with or work with or play with or eat with or go to school with or ride the bus with, or with whom they share a hospital ward or a prison cell block, any local concentration of the people most likely to display the behavior will enhance the likelihood that, at least in that locality, the activity will reach critical mass. Look back at Curve A. Cut off the top half of the diagram: just slice it horizontally at 50 on the vertical axis. The lower half of the diagram describes half the population—the half most easily induced to attend. Forget the top half; those people are now out of the picture. Next recalibrate the vertical axis so that it reads 100 percent where it used to read 50. And now because we've compressed the vertical scale but not the horizontal, replace the 45-degree line with a line of slope ½, a straight line going from the lower left to the upper right corner of our new rectangle. It cuts the A curve. Everywhere to the right of that intersection there are now more than enough people to sustain the activity.

By separating away half the population, and specifically the half least likely to attend, we have doubled the influence of everybody who attends—doubled the percentage that he or she represents. In this group we now have two equilibria, one with nobody attending and the other with everybody. By dividing the class into the more susceptible and the less susceptible halves, we have created a situation in which full attendance by half the class is sustainable.

Now look at the large-majority-equilibrium of Curve *B* and suppose we want to discourage attendance (or smoking, or whatever the activity is). Again divide the population into the more and the less susceptible halves by drawing that horizontal line halfway up the scale. Remove the bottom, more susceptible half. Recalibrate the top half of the vertical scale from zero to 100 and draw that straight line from the lower-left to the upper-right corner of this rectangle. The curve is everywhere beneath it; the activity will die away, or never get started. The people in the lower half are still doing it, but they were doing it anyway, and about 20 of the 70 who did it have stopped. Alternatively, if we like the activity and the two groups are separated, one attending fully and the other not at all, mixing them as a single population should induce another 20 or so to attend. If freshmen are the more susceptible and sophomores the less, and they are in separate classes of 50 each, the freshmen attending the Saturday class and the sophomores not, mixing them in one large class or mixing 25 of each in both classes should get about 20 sophomores attending.

The Commons

Some years ago Garrett Hardin chose a title that is insinuating its way into our common vocabulary to describe a motivational structure that is remarkably pervasive. He gave an address entitled "The Tragedy of the Commons" that was published in *Science* (Vol. 162, No. 3859, December 13, 1968, pp. 1243–48). References to the commons are showing up everywhere, and the term is beginning to serve the same shorthand purpose as words like "multiplier," "noise," "zero-sum," "critical-mass," or "bandwagon." A decade earlier "prisoner's dilemma" escaped the domain of game theory and became shorthand for a commonly occurring situation between two individuals, the one in which two people hurt each other more than they help themselves in making self-serving choices and could both be better off if obliged to choose the opposite. Hardin's common grazing grounds are a particular multi-person version of the same motivational structure.

The image is provocative. Every time one of us noses his car onto a crowded highway he is likely to be reminded of cattle overgrazing the common grassland. Soon, people at a meeting who have something worth saying, but not quite worth listening to, may begin to look like the cows that eat and trample the grass that another cow had its eye on. Economists have a long history of attention to the commons, and it is neither accident nor the unique genius of Garrett Hardin that that concept is now regularly applied to the dumping of sewage in a common waterway as well as the extraction of oil from a common pool or the killing of whales in a common sea, and even to a proliferating human population for which the earth and its resources have been likened to a common breeding ground.

"The commons" has come to serve as a paradigm for situations in which people so impinge on each other in pursuing their own interests that collectively they might be better off if they could be restrained, but no one gains individually by self-restraint. Common pasture in a village of England or Colonial New England was not only common property of the villagers but unrestrictedly available to their animals. The more cattle (or sheep or whatever) that were put to graze on the common, the less forage there was for each animal—and more of it got trampled—but as long as there was *any* profit in grazing one's animal on the common, villagers were motivated to do so. The benefit to the animal's owner would be less if there were 300 cattle than 200, and indeed the 300 might produce less meat or milk in total than 200 could on the same pasture; but a person who has two or three cows to put on the common is concerned with the meat and milk that his own cows produce, not with whether the average for all cows goes down 1 or 2 percent and total production in the village is smaller. And if he should reflect that all the cattle, including his own, together produce less than if he withdrew his two or three cows from the common, he knowns that the same is true of everybody's two or three cows, and his own are getting only what everybody else's cattle are getting.

The arithmetic might be like this: Suppose milk is what we produce. The first few cattle having the whole common to themselves produce a thousand quarts per cow per season; the size of the pasture is such that additional cows would steadily reduce production per cow until a thousand beasts on the common will survive but cannot produce milk. If the decline is linear—and that eases our arithmetic—200 cows would produce only 800 quarts apiece; 400 cows, 600; 600 cows, 400; and 800 cows, 200 quarts apiece. By calculating total production for successive hundreds we get 90,000 quarts from a hundred cows; 160,000 quarts from 200; 210,000 from 300; 240,000 from 400; and 250,000 from 500. With 600 cows, the total is down to 240,000; and then 210,000; 160,000; 90,000; and zero with a thousand cows. Together we could be better off slaughtering for their hides any cows in excess of 500, because together we get more milk from 500 cows than from 600. But even with 800 cows on the common my own cows are yielding 200 quarts, and if the pasture costs me nothing I can only lose 2,000 quarts of milk by removing my ten cows (even though all the other cows would gain more than 2,000 quarts if I did).

The commons are a special but widespread case out of a broader class of situations in which some of the costs or damages of what people do occur beyond their purview, and they either don't know or don't care about them. Pollution, infection, litter, noise, dangerous driving, carelessness with fire, and hoarding during a shortage often have that character. People may try to submit voluntarily to collective restraints on the behavior that is individually uninhibited but collectively costly.

It is useful to observe the particular characteristics of the problem of the commons, because it helps in comparative diagnosis. The model of the commons is widely and loosely used, and it is worthwhile to distinguish between the strict paradigm of the commons and the looser array of related models. Analytically, two noteworthy features of a common are that (1) only those who use the common are affected by the way it is used, and they are affected in proportion to how much they use it, and (2) the costs of using or over-using the common are in the same "currency" as the benefits, namely, a reduction in milk in our example. The paradigm fits better the class of problems called "congestion" or wasteful exploitation than to the problems identified with noise, pollution, and public safety. Non-pasture examples are the freeway so crowded that traffic moves barely faster than on the side streets, the beach so crowded that people wonder why they came, and the library so crowded that you'd do as well to buy your own books. Another is the common pool of petroleum into which dozens of independent oil companies drill their wells, pumping as fast as they can without regard to conservation because what each gets belongs to him and what he leaves is up for grabs.

Looser definitions of "the commons" will include situations that are similar but not identical in analytical structure. Hoarding library books, hogging pay telephones at a busy airport, sitting through intermission for fear of losing one's seat, and exercising tenure in a rent-controlled apartment when one would prefer to move but has no seniority elsewhere, are other examples of the "wasteful" collective use of scarce resources. Over-using wind, water, and land for the disposal of smoke, refuse, and liquid wastes is rather like over-using the local common sanitary landfill—a good example of the contemporary survival of the "common" in many parts of the country—but here the noxious consequences of over-use or careless use are not, as in the strict case of the commons, confined to others who also use or over-use or use carelessly. When I add my car to the congestion on the turnpike, the effect may be much like adding my cow to the common pasture, impeding the progress of other drivers on the turnpike; but my exhaust emissions will contribute to the eye and lung irritation of people who live nearby and do not use the turnpike (and other drivers in their air-conditioned cars may be least affected).

Noise and litter in the park or on the beach or by the roadside are close to the strict definition of the common—parks, beaches, and roadsides being literally free to common use and the main effects of noise and litter being on those who use those commons. Congested airports, like congested roads and beaches, are close analogs of the common; but the aircraft noise mainly affects people who live nearby, not users of the airport, and, unlike the transistor radio at the beach or in the public park, the airport noise belongs to that broader category of activities that impose on others, but not reciprocally on other users as in the commons.

The arithmetic of the commons distinguishes three intensities of use. Typically in grazing cattle, catching fish, visting the museum, driving on the highway, or even using the winds for smoke removal, there is some level of use that represents good economy: more would be lost than gained by restricting use; and although usage reduces the average benefit it increases the total benefit up to a point. (In our example, that was anything up to 500 cows.) Beyond that is the range in which every user still benefits but the aggregate benefits are reduced by the excessive use. Users could gain from a fair system of restriction, and anybody who increases his use inflicts losses on others that exceed his own gains. The dividing line between these two regions is not as easy to draw for a crowded museum as for milk production, and will be more complex if people differ more in their sensitivity to crowds than cows differ in the sensitivity of their milk production to the quality of forage, or if people differ more in the way their driving affects traffic jams than cows differ in the way they trample the grass.

The third level of intensity occurs when there are more than enough cows (a thousand in our example) to extinguish the value of the common—so many cars that the turnpike is no quicker than the side roads, so many people on the beach or in the concert hall that late arrivals take a look and go home; hardly anybody is better off than if he hadn't come. This is not only the point at which the entire value of the common has been virtually extinguished by overuse; it is also the point at which restraining *current* users would do little good because others would take their place at the first sign of positive value. To restrict present users of the turnpike to three days a week in rotation on grounds that they are all better off using it three-fifths as often with only three-fifths as much traffic, will do them no good if all those other people, previously repelled by the congested turnpike, now find it so attractive they reroute themselves and become the missing two-fifths who can slow the traffic to where the turnpike again offers no net attraction.

Self-fulfilling and Other Expectations

When I was a boy, German shepherds were known as "police dogs," and we were afraid of them. We had reason to be: they were unfriendly. But they must have been unfriendly partly because we were afraid and not friendly to them. And owners who wanted their dogs to be unfriendly, to protect their property, selected the dogs they knew we would be afraid of. Had we obstinately believed that police dogs were merely "shepherds," loyal but gentle, brusque with hearts of gold, we might have subverted the whole system by misreading the owners' signals and overwhelming the poor dogs with our inexhaustible affection.

Self-fulfilling prophecy is one of those descriptive terms that are so apt that they not only come initially into common use to describe the phenomena for which they were originally coined but go on to have a life of their own, losing touch with the original context and joining the common parlance to mean whatever they seem to mean. The general idea is that certain expectations are of such a character that they induce the kind of behavior that will cause the expectations to be fulfilled. "Prophecy" is just quaint enough to give the term some idiomatic flavor; it is not, of course, the prophecy itself that leads to its own fulfillment, but the expectations that lead, through a chain of events and interactions that may be short or long, to an outcome that conforms to the expectations. (An unheeded prophecy is not expected to have the power of self-confirmation.)

The original usage referred to a more restricted model of expectations and behavior than the range of mechanisms to which it is nowadays applied. Originally, the term was applied to beliefs—expectations, prophecies—held by whites about blacks, or by any dominant or majority group about minority or low-status people. The beliefs could lead to white behavior which would be conducive to black behavior which would then conform with the beliefs. For example, if a particular minority is considered incapable of holding responsible positions, they will not be hired for responsible positions; they will have no opportunity for experience in responsible positions; and, lacking any such experience, they may indeed be incapable. If particular handicapped people are considered incapable of operating certain kinds of machinery, and if it takes some training and experience to learn to operate it, they will never get the training and the experience, and will indeed be incapable. If college students are thought to be unkindly disposed toward the faculty or uncomfortable in the presence of the faculty, the faculty may become sufficiently estranged to generate that very attitude among students.

Already now we have three different models of self-confirming expectations. There is the unilateral process of believing something about people, behaving toward them in accordance with those beliefs, and causing the beliefs to be confirmed. There is the reciprocal case, in which faculty and students believe something of each other, or Arabs and Jews, or officers and enlisted men, and the reciprocated expectations generate reciprocated attitudes and behaviors in accordance with those expectations. (If each of us believes that the other will attack without warning at the first opportunity, each of us may feel it necessary in self-defense to attack without warning at the first opportunity.) And then there is the selective process, somewhat exemplified by choosing police dogs as watch

dogs, that leads people who occupy particular roles to be obsequious or gregarious because it is so widely expected of them
that only the obsequious or the gregarious would want the job
or would get into that role. If men think that prostitutes are
the only women who smoke in public, and if women know it
and especially if prostitutes know it, women may—or there was
a time when they would—confine their smoking to indoors.

The broader class of phenomena to which the "self-fulfilling" terminology applies does not depend on discrimination or
reciprocal distrust. If we all believe there is going to be a
coffee shortage, we can cause one by doing what people do
when they believe there is going to be a coffee shortage. In the
1930s when people believed that a bank was on the verge of
insolvency they hurried to withdraw their deposits, provoking
the insolvency they feared. If people believe that a candidate
for the nomination has little chance because he has no support,
he'll get little support and have little chance. If everybody
believes you have to go early to get a good seat, you will have
to go early to get a good seat. And if enough senators believe
that enough senators will vote against Judge Carswell to deny
his confirmation to the Supreme Court, enough senators may
in fact be ready to do so.

Even these cases can be subdivided further into at least
two distinct models. First are the cases in which the more it is
expected the more it will happen, whatever "it" is; the more
people who think everybody will show up on time, the more
people will show up on time; the more people who believe
that attendance will be poor at some festivity, or support will
be meager for some campaign, the poorer will be the attendance or the support for the campaign. The alternative case
involves "critical mass," and is an all-or-none affair. If the
larger the majority the more disadvantageous it is to be in the
minority, if the more likely a candidate's success the more
important it is to have supported the candidate early, if the
more people who think the bank will fail the more urgent it is
to withdraw funds before the failure, then everybody, expect-

ing everybody to hold those expectations and to behave accordingly, will have extreme expectations and cause an extreme outcome. Dramatic examples may have been the sudden collapse of the Batista regime in Cuba, the evacuation of French colonists after the withdrawal of the French army from Algeria in 1960, or the abandonment of homes and property by white minorities in several African countries in the expectation that everybody would expect everybody else to leave, and leave.

Next, we can loosen the definition still further and include the outcomes that result from expectations but do not necessarily confirm and conform to them. Consider the people who want to tip a little above average, to arrive a little ahead of the crowd, to pay slightly higher wages than their competitors, to grade their students above but only slightly above the average grade, or to display slightly more critical capacity than their colleagues in reviewing candidates for admission to graduate school. If everyone shares this motivation, and if everybody expects the same average behavior, they will systematically displace the average from where they thought it would be. We could call this the *self-displacing prophecy*. And if everybody not only shares this motivation but suspects everybody else does too, everybody will make allowance for everybody else's bias and adjust his own performance further, aggravating the displacement. Taxicab tips will stabilize at a level where, on the average, people can not afford to tip above average, but college grades will escalate forever.

Then we have the *self-negating prophecy*. If everybody believes that an event will be too crowded, and stays home, it won't be too crowded. If after a snowstorm the helicopter predicts on the radio that the traffic will be terrible, and people believe it, the streets will be clear. If the Republicans all believe that their candidate will win by a landslide they may not consider it necessary to go to the polls, and the land may not slide. If everybody expects everybody else to bring food but no drinks, everybody will bring drinks but no food.

From that last category we can develop the *self-equilibrating expectations*. If we all bring drinks and no food to the picnic this Saturday, having expected everybody else to bring food but no drinks, we might all turn around and bring food next Saturday because everybody brought drinks this Saturday, but we probably won't. We're likely to bring too much food or too many drinks, but not completely out at the extreme; the following week we have a smaller correction to make; and gradually we converge on a balance. Thereafter for sporadic reasons, such as a change in some of the people who come to the picnic, we may from time to time have an excess of food or an excess of drink, but there will be a tendency toward a compensating switch the following week. So what we may have is a set of *self-correcting expectations*. Maybe not— there is no guarantee that we won't go on flipflopping forever —but if the process, whatever it is, is frequent or continuous, and some of us can make compensating adjustments more readily than others, the reversals will be trends rather than flipflops, and the behavior as well as the expectations will become equilibrated.

Still another category can be called *self-confirming signals*. If cigarette smokers come to believe that mentholated cigarettes are in green and blue-green packages, rival manufacturers may find it advantageous to put mentholated and only mentholated cigarettes in packages of those colors. If it is widely believed that people go to a particular singles bar to be propositioned, just being there is a signal that reaches the people who, also being there, are receptive to the signal.

Self-enforcing Conventions

If everybody expects everybody to pass on the right, that's the side to pass on. If everybody expects nobody to applaud between the movements of a quartet, hardly anybody will.

Most one-way street signs need no enforcing by the police. The command—or suggestion—is self-enforcing. A feature of many rules is that, good rules or bad, they are better than no rules at all; and these conventions that coerce via expectations can be exceedingly helpful. (Imagine trying to get along without an alphabetical order!) But people can be trapped into self-enforcing rules that misdirect behavior. A bad system of one-way street signs is likely to be as self-enforcing as a good one. And a tradition that separates the women from the men or the whites from the blacks, the students from the faculty or the officers from the enlisted men, may be strongly self-enforcing even though one or both of the two groups deplore the tradition, and it may continue as long as conspicuous exceptions are an embarrassment.

The man who invented traffic signals had a genius for simplicity.[7] He saw that where two streets intersected there was confusion and lost time because people got in each other's way; and he discovered, probably by personal experience, that self-discipline and good will among travelers was not enough to straighten them out. Even the courteous lost time waiting for each other. And some who mistakenly thought it was their turn suffered collision.

With magnificent simplicity he divided all travelers into two groups, those moving east-west and those moving north-south. He put the traffic into an alternating pattern. Nobody needed tickets, or schedules, or reservations to cross the intersection. All necessary instructions could be reduced to a binary code in red and green lights; all travelers within the scope of the plan could see the signals; and a single alternating mechanism could activate both sets of lights. There was no need to plan the day in advance; neither the lights nor the travelers needed to be synchronized with any other activity. Nor was there need for enforcement: once travelers got used to the lights, they learned that it was dangerous to cross

[7] In this country credit goes to Garrett A. Morgan, who created an "automatic stop-sign" in 1923 and sold the rights to General Electric for $40,000, according to the biographical note in Russell L. Adams, *Great Negroes, Past and Present*, California State Department of Education, Sacramento, 1973.

against a flow of traffic that was proceeding with confidence. The lights created the kind of order in which non-compliance carried its own penalty. And there was impartial justice in the way the lights worked: unable to recognize individual travelers, the lights could hurt no one's feelings by not granting favoritism.

A social planner can usefully contemplate traffic signals. They remind us that, though planning is often associated with control, the crucial element is often coordination. People need to do the right things at the right time in relation to what others are doing. In fact, the most ingenious piece of planning ever introduced into society may have been our common scheme for synchronizing clocks and calendars. I do not set my watch at zero every morning on arising and let it run through the day on the decimal system; I have a watch just like yours, one that I coordinate with everybody else's at remarkably little cost. And I know nobody who cheats.

There is a great annual celebration of this accomplishment in early summer when, together, we set our watches ahead for daylight saving. For the government to order us to do everything an hour earlier would be an interference; it would confront everybody with discretionary decisions; we'd all have to check who had actually changed his schedule and who had not. But if we just set our watches ahead on the same night it all goes smoothly. And we haven't much choice.

Daylight saving itself is sweetly arbitrary. Why exactly one hour? When the ancients in the Middle East divided the day into an awkward twenty-four parts, by a duodecimal system that corresponds to the Zodiac and the pence in an old shilling (obstinately disregarding the ten fingers that most of us count by), was it because they looked forward a millennium or two and realized that urban industrial society would want to shift the phase of its daily activities by exactly one twenty-fourth? Like the chickens that conveniently lay eggs of just the size that goes with a cup of flour, did some teleological principle make the unit for counting time exactly equivalent to the nine holes of golf that have to be squeezed in before summer darkness?

I know a man who has calculated that clocks should be set ahead one hour and thirty-five minutes, and another whose habits make a forty-minute shift bring the sun over the yardarm at the right moment during his August vacation. I don't think they'll ever get a bill through the legislature—for the same reason that the sprinter who can do the fastest eighty-seven yards ever stop-watched cannot get a modest adjustment accepted by the Olympic Committee.

Traffic signals and daylight saving both reflect the compelling forces toward convergence in many social decisions. Weights and measures, the pitches of screws, decimal coinage, and right-hand drive are beyond the power of individual influence. Even for governments, few such decisions are as easily manipulated as the one about what time we get up in the summer. Clock technology makes daylight saving markedly easier than switching steering posts and road rigns to get all those cars on the other side of the road at the same moment. Coins circulate much more rapidly than screws and bolts; we'll be years working off the non-metric thread angles that we inherited in all of our durable hardware.

Decimal coinage and right-hand drive may be worth the collective effort. Calendar reform would probably work. Spelling reform has been successfully organized. But switching nationally to another language would require the authority of a despot, the fervor of a religious cause, or a confusion of tongues that leaves the focus of a new convergence open to manipulation.

The inertia of some of these social decisions is impressive and sometimes exasperating. The familiar English typewriter keyboard was determined before people learned to play the machine with both hands. Anyone who types could recommend improvements, and experiments have shown that there are superior keyboards that can be quickly learned. The cost of changing keys or even replacing machines would entail no great outlay, especially as typists on different floors of a building can type on different keyboards without disturbing each other. My children, though, apparently as long as they live, will use their ring fingers for letters more appropriate to the index.

Consider a problem akin to daylight saving but more complex, one that may be as far in the future as the design of the standard keyboard is in the past, but which we might wisely anticipate in view of the inertia displayed by some of these social choices. The five-day workweek is common in America, but people may elect to take more of our increased productivity in leisure and less in the things that money buys. The four-day workweek may then become attractive. There is no assurance that it will—the demand for material goods may prove to be elastic rather than inelastic—but there is no compelling reason to suppose that the trend toward shorter workweeks has reached its secular limit. (And if it has, the nine-hour day can still make the four-day workweek popular.) Which day of the week do you want off? Which day off do you think we'll end up getting?

There are at least three different questions here. First, as individuals, if it is to be another day off during the week, which day off would *one* of us like? Second, collectively, if we must all have the same day off, which day would we like universally treated as a second Saturday? And third, if we were betting on the shape of the workweek for the year 2030, how would we place our bets?

The first question is complicated. The day you'd prefer to have off may depend on what days other people have off. A weekday is great for going to the dentist unless the dentist takes the same day off. Friday is a great day to head for the country, avoiding Saturday traffic, unless everyone has Friday off. Tuesday is no good for going to the beach if Wednesday is the day the children have no school; but Tuesday is no good for getting away from the kids if that's the day they don't go to school. Staggered days are great for relieving the golf courses and the shopping centers; but it may demoralize teachers and classes to have a fifth of the children officially absent from school each day of the week, and may confuse families if the fourth-grader is home on Tuesday and the fifth-grader on Wednesday. And the children cannot very well go to school the day that the teacher isn't there, nor can the teacher go to the dentist on the day the dentist takes off to go to the beach with his children.

An important possibility is that we collectively like staggered workweeks, to relieve congestion and rush hours everywhere, but that we all slightly prefer to be among the 20 percent who choose Friday so that we can go to the dentist if we need to or get away for the long weekend if our teeth need no repair. If everyone feels that way, we shall not end up dispersing ourselves among the days of the week; instead, we shall all pick Friday—up to the point where Friday has become so congested that, all things considered, it is no better than Wednesday. The roads are jammed, the queues are long at the golf tees or the ski lifts, not enough stores are open to make shopping worthwhile; and we have collectively spoiled Friday with congestion. We have overcrowded Friday like a common grazing ground, by freely exercising our separate choices.

One can always hope for some ecological balance, some higher collective rationality, some goal-seeking evolutionary process. But it has not worked for staggered rush hours, which are substantially uninfluenced by government. And we seem legislatively unable to distribute Washington's Birthday town-by-town among the different weeks of February to smooth the peak loads for airlines and highway travel and ski-lift operation.

Meanwhile we can give thanks for small blessings, like our ability to synchronize daylight saving.

The Social Contract

A strange phenomenon on Boston's Southeast Expressway is reported by the traffic helicopter. If a freak accident, or a severe one, occurs in the southbound lane in the morning, it slows the northbound rush-hour traffic more than on the side where the obstruction occurs. People slow down to enjoy a look at the wreckage on the other side of the divider. Curiosity has the same effect as a bottleneck. Even the driver who, when he arrives at the site, is ten minutes behind schedule is likely to feel that he's paid the price of admission and, though the highway is at last clear in front of him, will not resume speed until he's had his look, too.

Eventually large numbers of commuters have spent an extra ten minutes driving for a ten-second look. (Ironically, the wreckage may have been cleared away, but they spend their ten seconds looking for it, induced by the people ahead of them who seemed to be looking at something.) What kind of a bargain is it? A few of them, offered a speedy bypass, might have stayed in line out of curiosity; most of them, after years of driving, know that when they get there what they're likely to see is worth about ten seconds' driving time. When they get to the scene, the ten minutes' delay is a sunk cost; their own sightseeing costs them only the ten seconds. It also costs ten seconds apiece to the three score motorists crawling along behind them.

Everybody pays his ten minutes and gets his look. But he pays ten seconds for his own look and nine minutes, fifty seconds for the curiosity of the drivers ahead of him.

It is a bad bargain.

More correctly, it is a bad result because there is no bargain. As a collective body, the drivers might overwhelmingly vote to maintain speed, each foregoing a ten-second look and each saving himself ten minutes on the freeway. Unorganized, they are at the mercy of a decentralized accounting system according to which no driver suffers the losses that he imposes on the people behind him.

Returning from Cape Cod on a Sunday afternoon, motorists were held up for a mile or more, at a creeping pace, by a mattress that had fallen off the top of some returning vacationer's station wagon. Nobody knows how many hundreds of cars slowed down a mile in advance, arrived at the mattress five minutes later, waited for the oncoming traffic, and swerved around before resuming speed. Somebody may eventually have halted on the shoulder just beyond the mattress and walked back to remove it from the traffic lane. If not, it may still have been there the following Sunday.

Again there was no bargain. Failing the appearance of a driver in a mood to do good—not a common mood on a hot highway with hungry children in the back seat—somebody would have had to be elected to the duty or compensated for performing it. Nobody gains by removing the mattress after he has passed it, and nobody can remove it until he has passed it.

Had the traffic helicopter been there, it might have proposed that each among the next hundred motorists flip a dime out the right-hand window to the person who removed the mattress as they went by. This would have given the road clearer a property right in the path he had opened, yielding a return on his investment and a benefit to the consumers behind him. But a long string of automobiles united only by a common journey, without voice communication or any way to organize a mobile town meeting as they approach the mattress, is unlikely to get organized. So we give thanks for the occasional occurrence of individual accounting systems that give a positive score for anonymous good turns.

Both the curiosity on the Southeast Expressway and the urge to get home once the mattress has been passed illustrate universal situations of individual decision and collective interest. People do things, or abstain from doing things, that affect others, beneficially or adversely. Without appropriate organization, the results may be pretty unsatisfactory. "Human nature" is easily blamed; but, accepting that most people are more concerned with their own affairs than with the affairs of others, and more aware of their own concerns than of the concerns of others, we may find human nature less pertinent than social organization. These problems often do have solutions. The solutions depend on some kind of social organization, whether that organization is contrived or spontaneous, permanent or ad hoc, voluntary or disciplined.

In the one case—pausing to look at the wreck—the problem is to get people to *abstain* from something that imposes costs on others. In the second case—yanking the mattress off the cement—the problem is to get somebody to take the trouble to *do* something that benefits himself not at all but will benefit others greatly.

Another distinction is that the first case involves *everybody*, the second *somebody*. We can easily turn the mattress case around and make it an act of carelessness that hurts others, not an act of good will for their benefit. Whoever tied the mattress carelessly may have considered the loss of the mattress in case the knot came loose, but not the risk that a thousand families would be late getting home behind him. So, also, on the Expressway we can drop our prejudices against morbid sightseeing and just suppose that people are driving comfortably along minding their business. They are in no great hurry but somebody behind them is, in fact a lot of people. It is worth a lot of time collectively, and maybe even money, to get the unhurried driver to bestir himself or to pick another route. He needn't feel guilty; he may even want something in return for giving up his right of way to people who like to drive faster. Without organized communication, he may know nothing about the hurry they are in behind him, and care even less.

A good part of social organization—of what we call society —consists of institutional arrangements to overcome these divergences between perceived individual interest and some larger collective bargain. Some of it is market-oriented—ownership, contracts, damage suits, patents and copyrights, promissory notes, rental agreements, and a variety of communications and information systems. Some have to do with government— taxes to cover public services, protection of persons, a weather bureau if weather information is not otherwise marketable, one-way streets, laws against littering, wrecking crews to clear away that car in the southbound lane and policemen to wave us on in the northbound lane. More selective groupings—the

union, the club, the neighborhood—can organize incentive systems or regulations to try to help people do what individually
they wouldn't but collectively they may wish to do. Our morals
can substitute for markets and regulations, in getting us sometimes to do from conscience the things that in the long run we
might elect to do only if assured of reciprocation.

What we are dealing with is the frequent divergence
between what people are individually motivated to do and
what they might like to accomplish together. Consider the
summer brown-out. We are warned ominously that unless we
all cut our use of electricity in midsummer we may overload
the system and suffer drastic consequences, sudden black-outs
or prolonged power failures, unpredictable in their consequences. In other years we are warned of water shortages;
leaky faucets account for a remarkable amount of waste, and
we are urged to fit them with new washers. There just cannot
be any question but what, for most of us if not all of us, we are
far better off if we all switch off the lights more assiduously,
cut down a little on the air-conditioning, repair the leaky faucets, let the lawns get a little browner and the cars a little dir-
tier, and otherwise reduce our claims on the common pool of
water and electric power. For if we do not, we suffer worse
and less predictably—the air-conditioner may be out altogether
on the hottest day, and all lights out just when we need them,
when overload occurs or some awkward emergency rationing
system goes into effect.

But turning down my air-conditioner, or turning the lights
out for five minutes when I leave the room, or fixing my leaky
faucet, can't do me any good. Mine is an infinitesimal part of
the demand for water and electricity, and while the minute
difference that I can make is multiplied by the number of
people to whom it can make a difference, the effect on me of
what I do is truly negligible.

Within the family we can save hot water on Friday night
by taking brief showers, rather than racing to be first in the
shower and use it all up. But that may be because within the

family we care about each other, or have to pretend we do, or can watch each other and have to account for the time we stand enjoying the hot water. It is harder to care about, or to be brought to account by, the people who can wash their cars more effectively if I let my lawn burn, or who can keep their lawns greener if I leave my car dirty.

What we need in these circumstances is an enforceable social contract. I'll cooperate if you and everybody else will. I'm better off if we all cooperate than if we go our separate ways. In matters of great virtue and symbolism, especially in emergencies, we can become imbued with a sense of solidarity and abide by a golden rule. We identify with the group, and we act as we hope everybody will act. We enjoy rising to the occasion, rewarded by a sense of virtue and community. And indeed a good deal of social ethics is concerned with rules of behavior that are collectively rewarding if collectively obeyed (even though the individual may not benefit from his own participation). But if there is nothing heroic in the occasion; if what is required is a protracted nuisance; if one feels no particular community with great numbers of people who have nothing in common but connected water pipes; if one must continually decide what air-conditioned temperature to allow himself in his own bedroom, or whether to go outdoors and check the faucet once again; and especially if one suspects that large numbers of people just are not playing the game—most people may cooperate only halfheartedly, and many not at all. And then when they see the dribbling faucet from which the pressure is gone, or read that the electrical shortage is undiminished in spite of exhortations to turn off the air-conditioners, even that grudging participation is likely to be abandoned.

The frustration is complete when a homeowner, stepping onto his back porch at night, cocks his head and hears the swish of invisible lawn sprinkers in the darkness up and down the block. He damns the lack of enforcement and turns the handle on his own sprinkler, making the violation unanimous.

There is no inconsistency in what he damned and what he did. He wants the ban enforced; but if it is not enforced he intends to water his lawn, especially if everybody else is doing it. He's not interested in doing minute favors for a multitude of individuals, most of whom he doesn't know, letting his lawn go to ruin; he *is* willing to enter a bargain, letting his lawn go to ruin if they will let theirs go the same way, so that they can all have unrestricted use of their showers, washing machines, toilets, and sinks.

The trouble is often in making the bargain stick. Water meters capable of shifting gears at peak-load times of day, with weekly water rates or water rations publicized through the summer, would undoubtedly take care of the problem. But fancy meters are expensive; fluctuating rates are a nuisance and hard to monitor; large families with lots of dirty clothes to wash will complain at the rates while a childless couple can afford to wash its new car. Moreover, long before an acceptable "solution" has been devised and publicized, a wet, cold autumn ensues and the problem now is to devise a scheme of mandatory snow tires on select roads in time for that unexpected early snowstorm that snarls everything up because my car, skidding sideways on a hill, blocks your car and all the cars behind you. In waiting to get my snow tires at the after-Christmas sales, I was gambling your dinner hour against the price of my tires.

Sometimes it takes only a fraction of us to solve the worst of the problem. If the electrical overload that threatens is only a few percent, half of us may find a way to enforce a voluntary restriction, and thus avoid the breakdown. It infuriates us that the other half don't do their share. It especially infuriates us if the other half, relieved of whatever anxiety might have made them a little more conscious of wasted electricity, now relax and leave their lights on in the comfortable knowledge that, to prevent black-out, we have turned off our electric fans. Still, if we don't charge too much for spite, it can be a good bargain even for the half of us that carry the whole load. The "free riders" are better off than we are, but as the cooperative half we may be better off for having found a way to make ourselves cut back in unison.

Sometimes it won't work unless nearly everybody plays the game. Trashcans in our nation's capital say that "Every Litter Bit Hurts," but it is really the first litter bits that spoil a park or sidewalk. Ten times as much makes it worse, but not ten times worse. It takes only one power mower to turn a quiet Sunday morning into the neighborhood equivalent of a stamping mill; indeed, the speed with which a few timid homeowners light up their machines, once the first brazen neighbor has shattered the quiet with his own three-and-a-half horsepower, suggests that they expect no reproach once it's clear that it's beyond their power to provide a quiet Sunday by merely turning off one machine among several.

Morality and virtue probably work this way. Whatever the technology of cooperative action—whether every litter bit hurts, or the first few bits just about spoil everything—people who are willing to do their part as long as everybody else does, living by a commonly shared golden rule, enjoying perhaps the sheer participation in a common preference for selflessness, may have a limited tolerance to the evidence or to the mere suspicion that others are cheating on the social contract, bending the golden rule, making fools of those who carefully minimize the detergent they send into the local river or who carry away the leaves they could so easily have burned.

There are the cases, though, in which not everybody gains under the social contract. Some gain more than others, and some not enough to compensate for what they give up. An agreement to turn off air-conditioners, to make sure that electric lights and the more essential appliances can keep functioning, may be a bad bargain for the man or woman with hay fever, who'd rather have a dry nose in darkness than sneeze with the lights on. A ban on outdoor uses of water may be a crude but acceptable bargain for most people, but not for the couple whose joy and pride is their garden. A sudden police order to go full speed past that accident on the Expressway is a welcome relief to the people who still have a mile or so to crawl before they get to the scene of the accident; drivers who have been crawling for ten minutes and are just at the point of having a good look will be annoyed. Ten minutes ago they would not have been; but ten minutes go somebody ahead of them would have been.

If participation requires unanimous consent, it may be necessary and it may be possible to compensate, for their participation, those to whom the advantages do not cover the costs. Compensation does complicate the arrangements, though, and when that couple who love their garden get paid for seeing it wither, their neighbors will suddenly discover how much they loved their own gardens.

In economics the most familiar cases of this general phenomenon involve some resource or commodity that is scarce, inelastic in supply, but freely available to all comers until the supply has run out. The most striking case was the buffalo, twenty or thirty million of whom roamed the plains west of the Mississippi at the end of the Civil War. As meat they were not marketable; rail transport of live animals had not reached the west. Their tongues were delicious and drew a high price, and for several years there was a thriving business in buffalo tongues, each of which left behind a thousand pounds of rotting meat. Then the hides became marketable and that was the end; twenty billion pounds of live meat was turned to rotting carcasses in the course of half a dozen years. Wagon trains detoured to avoid the stench of decaying buffaloes; and, roughly, for every five pounds of buffalo meat left on the ground, somebody got a penny for the hide. At any plausible interest rate the buffalo would have been worth more as live meat fifteen years later, when marketing became feasible, but to the hunter who killed fifty a day for their hides, it was that or nothing. There was no way that he could claim a cow and market his property right in her offspring fifteen years later.

Whales and electricity, buffaloes and the water supply:

scarce to the community but "free" to the individual as long as they last. In the small, the same phenomenon occurs when half a dozen businessmen tell the waiter to put it all on a single check; why save $6 for the group by having hamburger, when the steak costs the man who orders it only $1 more? People drink more at a party where the drinks are free and everybody is assessed his fraction of the total cost afterwards; it's a great way to get people to drink more than they can afford, and conviviality may recommend it. The manager of a club would have to be out of his mind, however, to propose that each month's total dining room budget be merely divided equally among all the members.

4

SORTING AND MIXING:
RACE AND SEX

P<small>EOPLE</small> <small>GET</small> <small>SEPARATED</small> along many lines and in many ways. There is segregation by sex, age, income, language, religion, color, personal taste, and the accidents of historical location. Some segregation results from the practices of organizations. Some is deliberately organized. Some results from the interplay of individual choices that discriminate. Some of it results from specialized communication systems, like languages. And some segregation is a corollary of other modes of segregation: residence is correlated with job location and transport.

If blacks exclude whites from their church, or whites exclude blacks, the segregation is organized; and it may be reciprocal or one-sided. If blacks just happen to be Baptists and whites Methodists, the two colors will be segregated Sunday morning whether they intend to be or not. If blacks join a black church because they are more comfortable among their own color, and whites a white church for the same reason, undirected individual choice can lead to segregation. And if the church bulletin board is where people advertise rooms for rent, blacks will rent rooms from blacks and whites from whites because of a communication system that is connected with churches that are correlated with color.

Some of the same mechanisms segregate college professors. The college may own some housing, from which all but college staff are excluded. Professors choose housing commensurate with their incomes, and houses are clustered by price while professors are clustered by income. Some professors prefer an academic neighborhood; any differential in professorial density will cause them to converge and increase the local density, and attract more professors. And house-hunting professors learn about available housing from colleagues and their spouses, and the houses they learn about are naturally the ones in neighborhood where professors already live.

The similarity ends there, and nobody is about to propose a commission to desegregate academics. Professors are not much missed by those they escape from in their residential choices. They are not much noticed by those they live among, and, though proportionately concentrated, are usually a minority in their neighborhood. While indeed they escape classes of people they would not care to live among, they are more conscious of where they do live than of where they don't, and the active choice is more like congregation than segregation, though the result may not be so different.

This chapter is about the kind of segregation—or separation, or sorting—that can result from discriminatory individual behavior. By "discriminatory" I mean reflecting an awareness, conscious or unconscious, of sex or age or religion or color or whatever the basis of segregation is, an awareness that influences decisions on where to live, whom to sit by, what occupation to join or to avoid, whom to play with, or whom to talk to. It examines some of the *individual* incentives and individual perceptions of difference that can lead *collectively* to segregation. It also examines the extent to which inferences can be drawn from actual collective segregation about the preferences of individuals, the strengths of those preferences, and the facilities for exercising them.

The main concern is segregation by "color" in the United States. The analysis, though, is so abstract that any twofold distinction could constitute an interpretation—whites and blacks, boys and girls, officers and enlisted men, students and faculty. The only requirement of the analysis is that the distinction be twofold, exhaustive, and recognizable. (Skin color, of course, is neither dichotomous nor even unidimensional, but by convention the distinction is nearly twofold, even in the United States census.)

At least two main processes of segregation are outside this analysis. One is organized action—legal or illegal, coercive or merely exclusionary, subtle or flagrant, open or covert, kindly or malicious, moralistic or pragmatic. The other is the process, largely but not entirely economic, by which the poor get separated from the rich, the less educated from the more educated, the unskilled from the skilled, the poorly dressed from the well dressed—in where they work and live and eat and play, in whom they know and whom they date and whom they go to school with. Evidently color is correlated with income, and income with residence; so even if residential choices were color-blind and unconstrained by organized discrimination, whites and blacks would not be randomly distributed among residences.

It is not easy to draw the lines separating "individually motivated" segregation from the more organized kind or from the economically induced kind. Habit and tradition are substitutes for organization. Fear of sanctions can coerce behavior whether or not the fear is justified, and whether the sanctions are consensual, conspiratorial, or dictated. Common expectations can lead to concerted behavior.

The economically induced separation is also intermixed with discrimination. To choose a neighborhood is to choose neighbors. To pick a neighborhood with good schools, for example, is to pick a neighborhood of *people* who want good schools. People may furthermore rely, even in making economic choices, on information that is color-discriminating; believing that darker-skinned people are on the average poorer than lighter-skinned, one may consciously or unconsciously rely on color as an index of poverty or, believing that others rely on color as an index, adopt their signals and indices accordingly.

For all these reasons, the lines dividing the individually motivated, the collectively enforced, and the economically induced segregation are not clear lines at all. They are furthermore not the only mechanisms of segregation. Separate or specialized communication systems—especially distinct languages —can have a strong segregating influence that, though interacting with the three processes mentioned, is nevertheless a different one.

Individual Incentives and Collective Results

Economists are familiar with systems that lead to aggregate results that the individual neither intends nor needs to be aware of, results that sometimes have no recognizable counterpart at the level of the individual. The creation of money by a commercial banking system is one; the way savings decisions cause depressions or inflations is another.

Biological evolution is responsible for a lot of sorting and separating, but the little creatures that mate and reproduce and forage for food would be amazed to know that they were bringing about separation of species, territorial sorting, or the extinction of species. Among social examples, the coexistence or extinction of second languages is a phenomenon that, though affected by decrees and school curricula, corresponds to no conscious collective choice.

Romance and marriage, as emphasized in Chapter 1, are exceedingly individual and private activities, at least in this country, but their genetic consequences are altogether aggregate. The law and the church may constrain us in our choices, and some traditions of segregation are enormously coercive; but, outside of royal families, there are few marriages that are part of a genetic plan. When a short boy marries a tall girl, or a blonde a brunette, it is no part of the individual's purpose to increase genetic randomness or to change some frequency distribution within the population.

Some of the phenomena of segregation may be similarly complex in relation to the dynamics of individual choice. One might even be tempted to suppose that some "unseen hand" separates people in a manner that, though foreseen and intended by no one, corresponds to some consensus or collective preference or popular will. But in economics we know a great many macro-phenomena, like depression and inflation, that do not reflect any universal desire for lower incomes or higher prices. The same applies to bank failures and market crashes. What goes on in the "hearts and minds" of small savers has little to do with whether or not they cause a depression. The hearts and minds and motives and habits of millions of people who participate in a segregated society may or may not bear close correspondence with the massive results that collectively they can generate.

A special reason for doubting any social efficiency in aggregate segregation is that the range of choice is often so meager. The demographic map of almost any American metropolitan area suggests that it is easy to find residential areas that are all white or nearly so and areas that are all black or nearly so but hard to find localities in which neither whites nor nonwhites are more than, say, three-quarters of the total. And, comparing decennial maps, it is nearly impossible to find an area that, if integrated within that range, will remain integrated long enough for a couple to get their house paid for or their children through school.

Some Quantitative Constraints

Counting blacks and whites in a residential block or on a baseball team will not tell how they get along. But it tells something, especially if numbers and ratios matter to the people who are moving in or out of the block or being recruited for the team. With quantitative analysis there are a few logical constraints, analogous to the balance-sheet identities in economics. (Being logical constraints, they contain no news unless one just never thought of them before.)

The simplest constraint on dichotomous mixing is that, within a given set of boundaries, not both groups can enjoy numerical superiority. For the whole population the numerical ratio is determined at any given time; but locally, in a city or a neighborhood, a church or a school or a restaurant, either blacks or whites can be a majority. But if each insists on being a local majority, there is only one mixture that will satisfy them—complete segregation.

Relaxing the condition, if whites want to be at least three-fourths and blacks at least one-third, it won't work. If whites want to be at least two-thirds and blacks no fewer than one-fifth, there is a small range of mixtures that meet the conditions. And not everybody can be in the mixtures if the overall ratio is outside the range.

In spatial arrangements, like a neighborhood or a hospital ward, everybody is next to somebody. A neighborhood may be 10 percent black or white; but if you have a neighbor on either side, the minimum nonzero percentage of opposite color is 50. If people draw their boundaries differently we can have everybody in a minority: at dinner, with men and women seated alternately, everyone is outnumbered two to one locally by the opposite sex but can join a three-fifths majority if he extends his horizon to the next person on either side.

Separating Mechanisms

The simple mathematics of ratios and mixtures tells us something about what outcomes are logically possible, but tells us little about the behavior that leads to, or that leads away from, particular outcomes. To understand what kinds of segregation or integration may result from individual choice, we have to look at the processes by which various mixtures and separations are brought about. We have to look at the incentives and the behavior that the incentives motivate, and particularly the way that different individuals comprising the society impinge on each other's choices and react to each other's presence.

There are many different incentives or criteria by which blacks and whites, or boys and girls, become separated. Whites may simply prefer to be among whites and blacks among blacks. Alternatively, whites may merely avoid or escape blacks and blacks avoid or escape whites. Whites may prefer the company of whites, while the blacks don't care. Whites may prefer to be among whites and blacks also prefer to be among whites, but if the whites can afford to live or to eat or to belong where the blacks cannot afford to follow, separation can occur.

Whites and blacks may not mind each other's presence, may even prefer integration, but may nevertheless wish to avoid minority status. Except for a mixture at exactly 50:50, no mixture will then be self-sustaining because there is none without a minority, and if the minority evacuates, complete segregation occurs. If both blacks and whites can tolerate minority status but place a limit on how small the minority is—for example, a 25 percent minority—initial mixtures ranging from 25 percent to 75 percent will survive but initial mixtures more extreme than that will lose their minority members and become all of one color. And if those who leave move to where they constitute a majority, they will increase the majority there and may cause the other color to evacuate.

Evidently if there are lower limits to the minority status that either color can tolerate, and if complete segregation obtains initially, no individual will move to an area dominated by the other color. Complete segregation is then a stable equilibrium.

Sorting and Scrambling

Minor-league players at Dodgertown—the place where Dodger-affiliated clubs train in the spring—are served cafeteria-style. "A boy takes the first seat available," according to the general manager. "This has been done deliberately. If a white boy doesn't want to eat with a colored boy, he can go out and buy his own food. We haven't had any trouble."[8]

Major-league players are not assigned seats in their dining hall; and though mixed tables are not rare, they are not the rule either. If we suppose that major- and minor-league racial attitudes are not strikingly different, we may conclude that

[8] Charles Maher, "The Negro Athlete in America," *The Los Angeles Times* Sports Section, March 29, 1968.

racial preference in the dining hall is positive but less than
the price of the nearest meal.

Actually, though, there is an alternative: whites and blacks
in like-colored clusters can enter the line together and, once
they have their trays, innocently take the next seats alongside
each other. Evidently they don't. If they did, some scrambling
system would have had to be invented. Maybe we conclude,
then, that the racial preferences, though enough to make separate eating the general rule, are not strong enough to induce
the slight trouble of picking partners before getting food. Or
perhaps we conclude that players lack the strategic foresight
to beat the cafeteria line as a seat-scrambling device.

But even a minor-league player knows how to think ahead
a couple of outs in deciding whether a sacrifice fly will
advance the ball team. It is hard to believe that if a couple of
players wanted to sit together it would not occur to them to
meet at the beginning of the line; and the principle extends
easily to segregation by color.

We are left with some alternative hypotheses. One is that
players are relieved to have an excuse to sit without regard to
color, and cafeteria-line–scrambling eliminates an embarrassing choice. Another is that players can ignore, accept, or even
prefer mixed tables but become uncomfortable or self-conscious, or think that others are uncomfortable or self-conscious,
when the mixture is lopsided. Joining a table with blacks and
whites is a casual thing, but being the seventh at a table with
six players of opposite color imposes a threshold of self-con-
sciousness that spoils the easy atmosphere and can lead to
complete and sustained separation.

Hostesses are familiar with the problem. Men and women
mix nicely at stand-up parties until, partly at random and
partly because a few men or women get stuck in a specialized
conversation, some clusters form that are nearly all male or all
female; selective migration then leads to the cocktail-party
equivalent of the Dodgertown major-league dining hall. Hostesses, too, have their equivalent of the cafeteria-line rule: they

alternate sexes at the dinner table, grasp people by the elbows and move them around the living room, or bring in coffee and make people serve themselves to disturb the pattern.

Sometimes the problem is the other way around. It is usually good to segregate smokers from non-smokers in planes and other enclosed public places; swimmers and surfers should be segregated in the interest of safety; and an attempt is made to keep slow-moving vehicles in the right-hand lane of traffic. Many of these dichotomous groupings are asymmetrical: cigar smokers are rarely bothered by people who merely breathe; the surfer dislikes having his board hit anybody in the head but there is somebody else who dislikes it much more; and the driver of a slow truck passing a slower one on a long grade is less conscious of who is behind him than the driver behind is of the truck in front. Styles of behavior differ: surfers like to be together and cluster somewhat in the absence of regulation; water-skiers prefer dispersal and are engaged in a mobile sport, and rarely reach accommodation with swimmers on how to share the water.

These several processes of separation, segregation, sharing, mixing, dispersal—sometimes even pursuit—have a feature in common. The consequences are aggregate but the decisions are exceedingly individual. The swimmer who avoids the part of the beach where the surfers are clustered, and the surfer who congregates where the surfboards are, are reacting individually to an environment that consists mainly of other individuals who are reacting likewise. The results can be unintended, even unnoticed. Non-smokers may concentrate in the least smoky railroad car; as that car becomes crowded, smokers, choosing less crowded cars, find themselves among smokers, whether they notice it or not, and less densely crowded, whether they appreciate it or not.

The more crucial phenomena are of course residential decisions and others, like occupational choice, inter-city migration, school- and church-population, where the separating and mixing involve lasting associations that matter. The minor-league players who eat lunch at Dodgertown have no cafeteria-line–mechanism to scramble their home addresses; and even if they were located at random, they would usually not be casually integrated, because mixed residential areas are few and the choice, for a black or for a white, is between living among blacks or living among whites—unless even that choice is restricted.

It is not easy to tell from the aggregate phenomenon just what the motives are behind the individual decisions, or how strong they are. The smoker on an airplane may not know that the person in front of him is sensitive to tobacco smoke; the water-skier might be willing to stay four hundred yards offshore if doing so didn't just leave a preferred strip to other skiers. The clustered men and women at that cocktail party may be bored and wish the hostess could shake things up, but without organization no one can do any good by himself. And people who are happy to work where English and French are both spoken may find it uncomfortable if their own language falls to extreme minority status; and by withdrawing they only aggravate the situation that induced them to withdraw.

People who have to choose between polarized extremes—a white neighborhood or a black, a French-speaking club or one where English alone is spoken, a school with few whites or one with few blacks—will often choose in the way that reinforces the polarization. Doing so is no evidence that they prefer segregation, only that, if segregation exists and they have to choose between exclusive association, people elect like rather than unlike environments.

The dynamics are not always transparent. There are chain reactions, exaggerated perceptions, lagged responses, speculation on the future, and organized efforts that may succeed or fail. Three people of a particular group may break leases and move out of an apartment without being noticed, but if they do it the same week somebody will notice and comment. Other residents are then alerted to whether the whites or the blacks or the elderly, or the families with children or the families without, are moving away, thereby generating the situation of minority status they thought they foresaw.

Some of the processes may be passive, systemic, unmotivated but nevertheless biased. If job vacancies are filled by word of mouth or apartments go to people who have acquaintances in the building, or if boys can marry only girls they know and can know only girls who speak their language, a biased communication system will preserve and enhance the prevailing homogeneities.

A Self-Forming Neighborhood Model

Some vivid dynamics can be generated by any reader with a half-hour to spare, a roll of pennies and a roll of dimes, a tabletop, a large sheet of paper, a spirit of scientific inquiry, or, lacking that spirit, a fondness for games.

Get a roll of pennies, a roll of dimes, a ruled sheet of paper divided into one-inch squares, preferably at least the size of a checkerboard (sixty-four squares in eight rows and eight columns) and find some device for selecting squares at random. We place dimes and pennies on some of the squares, and suppose them to represent the members of two homogeneous groups—men and women, blacks and whites, French-speaking and English-speaking, officers and enlisted men, students and faculty, surfers and swimmers, the well dressed and the poorly dressed, or any other dichotomy that is exhaustive and recognizable. We can spread them at random or put them in contrived patterns. We can use equal numbers of dimes and pennies or let one be a minority. And we can stipulate various rules for individual decision.

For example, we can postulate that every dime wants at least half its neighbors to be dimes, every penny wants a third of its neighbors to be pennies, and any dime or penny whose immediate neighborhood does not meet these conditions gets up and moves. Then by inspection we locate the ones that are due to move, move them, keep on moving them if necessary and, when everybody on the board has settled down, look to see what pattern has emerged. (If the situation never "settles down," we look to see what kind of endless turbulence or cyclical activity our postulates have generated.)

Define each individual's neighborhood as the eight squares surrounding him; he is the center of a 3-by-3 neighborhood. He is content or discontent with his neighborhood according to the colors of the occupants of those eight surrounding squares, some of which may be empty. We furthermore suppose that, if he is discontent with the color of his own neighborhood, he moves to the nearest empty square that meets his demands.

As to the order of moves, we can begin with the discontents nearest the center of the board and let them move first, or start in the upper left and sweep downward to the right, or let the dimes move first and then the pennies; it usually turns out that the precise order is not crucial to the outcome.

Then we choose an overall ratio of pennies to dimes, the two colors being about equal or one of them being a "minority." There are two different ways we can distribute the dimes and the pennies. We can put them in some prescribed pattern that we want to test, or we can spread them at random.

Start with equal numbers of dimes and pennies and suppose that the demands of both are "moderate"—each wants something more than one-third of his neighbors to be like himself. The number of neighbors that a coin can have will be anywhere from zero to eight. We make the following specifications. If a person has one neighbor, he must be the same color; of two neighbors, one must be his color; of three, four, or five neighbors, two must be his color; and of six, seven, or eight neighbors, he wants at least three.

It is possible to form a pattern that is regularly "integrated" that satisfies everybody. An alternating pattern does it (Figure 3), on condition that we take care of the corners.

SORTING AND MIXING: RACE AND SEX

```
      #  O  #  O  #  O
   #  O  #  O  #  O  #  O
   O  #  O  #  O  #  O  #
   #  O  #  O  #  O  #  O
   O  #  O  #  O  #  O  #
   #  O  #  O  #  O  #  O
   O  #  O  #  O  #  O  #
      O  #  O  #  O  #
```

Figure 3

No one can move, except to a corner, because there are no other vacant cells; but no one wants to move. We now mix them up a little, and in the process empty some cells to make movement feasible.

There are 60 coins on the board. We remove 20, using a table of random digits; we then pick 5 empty squares at random and replace a dime or a penny with a 50-50 chance. The result is a board with 64 cells, 45 occupied and 19 blank. Forty individuals are just where they were before we removed 20 neighbors and added 5 new ones. The left side of Figure 4 shows one such result, generated by exactly this process. The #'s are dimes and the O's are pennies; alternatively, the #'s speak French and the O's speak English, the #'s are black and the O's are white, the #'s are boys and the O's are girls, or whatever you please.

```
_  #  _  #  O  #  _  O        _  _  _  #  _  #  _  _
#  #  #  O  _  O  #  O        _  _  _  _  _  _  _  _
_  #  O  _  _  #  O  #        _  _  _  _  _  _  _  _
_  O  #  O  #  O  #  O        _  _  #  _  #  _  #  _
O  O  O  #  O  O  O  _        _  _  _  _  _  _  _  _
#  _  #  #  #  _  _  O        #  _  _  _  _  _  _  _
_  #  O  #  O  #  O  _        _  _  O  _  O  _  O  _
_  O  _  O  _  _  #  _        _  _  _  _  _  _  _  _
```

Figure 4

The right side of Figure 4 identifies the individuals who are not content with their neighborhoods. Six #'s and three O's want to move; the rest are content as things stand. The pattern is still "integrated"; even the discontent are not without some neighbors like themselves, and few among the content are without neighbors of opposite color. The general pattern is not strongly segregated in appearance. One is hard-put to block out #-neighborhoods or O-neighborhoods at this stage. The problem is to satisfy a fraction, 9 of 45, among the #'s and O's by letting them move somewhere among the 19 blank cells.

Anybody who moves leaves a blank cell that somebody can move into. Also, anybody who moves leaves behind a neighbor or two of his own color; and when he leaves a neighbor, his neighbor loses a neighbor and may become discontent. Anyone who moves gains neighbors like himself, adding a neighbor like them to their neighborhood but also adding one of opposite color to the unlike neighbors he acquires.

I cannot too strongly urge you to get the dimes and pennies and do it yourself. I can show you an outcome or two. A computer can do it for you a hundred times, testing variations in neighborhood demands, overall ratios, sizes of neighborhoods, and so forth. But there is nothing like tracing it through for yourself and seeing the thing work itself out. In an hour you can do it several times and experiment with different rules of behavior, sizes and shapes of boards, and (if you turn some of the coins heads and some tails) subgroups of dimes and pennies that make different demands on the color compositions of their neighborhoods.

Chain Reaction

What is instructive about the experiment is the "unraveling" process. Everybody who selects a new environment affects the environments of those he leaves and those he moves among. There is a chain reaction. It may be quickly damped,

with little motion, or it may go on and on and on with striking
results. (The results of course are only suggestive, because few
of us live in square cells on a checkerboard.)

One outcome for the situation depicted in Figure 4 is
shown in Figure 5. It is "one outcome" because I have not
explained exactly the order in which individuals moved. If the
reader reproduces the experiment himself, he will get a
slightly different configuration, but the general pattern will not
be much different. Figure 6 is a replay from Figure 4, the only
difference from Figure 5 being in the order of moves. It takes
a few minutes to do the experiment again, and one quickly
gets an impression of the kind of outcome to expect. Changing
the neighborhood demands, or using twice as many dimes as
pennies, will drastically affect the results; but for any given set
of numbers and demands, the results are fairly stable.

All the people are content in Figures 5 and 6. And they are
more segregated. This is more than just a visual impression:
we can make a few comparisons. In Figure 4 the O's altogether
had as many O's for neighbors as they had #'s; some had
more or less than the average, and 3 were discontent. For the
#'s the ratio of #-neighbors to O-neighbors was 1:1, with a
little colony of #'s in the upper left corner and 6 widely distributed discontents. After sorting themselves out in Figure 5,
the average ratio of like to unlike neighbors for #'s and O's

```
     # #    O # #            # # # O        O
 # # # O O O # #         # # # O    O    O
 # # O O        O #      # # O           O
 # O    O    O O O       O    O    O    O
 O O O # O O O           O O O # O O O
   O # # # O O O             # # # O O O
     # # # #             O # # # # # # #
 O O            #        O O        # # #
```

| Figure 5 | Figure 6 |

together was 2.3:1, more than double the original ratio. And it
is about triple the ratio that any individual demanded! Figure
6 is even more extreme. The ratio of like to unlike neighbors is
2.8:1, nearly triple the starting ratio and four times the minimum demanded.

Another comparison is the number who had no opposite
neighbors in Figure 4. Three were in that condition before
people started moving; in Figure 5 there are 8 without neighbors of opposite color, and in Figure 6 there are 14.

What can we conclude from an exercise like this? We may
at least be able to disprove a few notions that are themselves
based on reasoning no more complicated than the checkerboard. Propositions beginning with "It stands to reason that . . ."
can sometimes be discredited by exceedingly simple demonstrations that, though perhaps true, they do not exactly "stand
to reason." We can at least persuade ourselves that certain
mechanisms could work, and that observable aggregate phenomena could be compatible with types of "molecular movement" that do not closely resemble the aggregate outcomes
that they determine.

There may be a few surprises. What happens if we raise
the demands of one color and lower the demands of the other?
Figure 7 shows typical results. Here we increased by one the
number of like neighbors that a # demanded and decreased

```
# # # # O       O
# # # # O O     O
# # # #       O
  O # O O O     O
O O O # O O O
      # # O
    O # # # O
  O   O # # #
```

Figure 7

by one the number that an *O* demanded, as compared with Figures 5 and 6. By most measures, "segregation" is about the same as in Figures 5 and 6. The difference is in population densities: the *O*'s are spread out all over their territory, while the #'s are packed in tight. The reader will discover, if he actually gets those pennies and dimes and tries it for himself, that something similar would happen if the demands of the two colors were equal but one color outnumbered the other by two or three to one. The minority then tends to be noticeably more tightly packed. Perhaps from Figure 7 we could conclude that if surfers mind the presence of swimmers less than swimmers mind the presence of surfers, they will become almost completely separated, but the surfers will enjoy a greater expanse of water.

Is it "Segregated"?

The reader might try guessing what set of individual preferences led from Figure 4 to the pattern in Figure 8.

The ratio of like to unlike neighbors for all the #'s and *O*'s together is slightly more than three to one; and there are 6 *O*'s and 8 #'s that have no neighbors of opposite color. The result is evidently segregation; but, following a suggestion of my dictionary, we might say that the process is one of *aggregation*,

```
    # #         # #
  # # #       # # #
  # # O O O # O
      O O O O O O O
  O O O # O O O
      O # # # O O O
      # # #     O O
      # #
```

Figure 8

because the rules of behavior ascribed both to #'s and to O's in Figure 8 were simply that each would move to acquire three neighbors of like color irrespective of the presence or absence of neighbors of opposite color. As an individual motivation, this is quite different from the one that formed the patterns in Figures 5 and 6. But in the aggregate it may be hard to discern which motivation underlies the pattern, and the process, of segregated residence. And it matters!

The first impact of a display like this on a reader may be—unless he finds it irrelevant—discouragement. A moderate urge to avoid small-minority status may cause a nearly integrated pattern to unravel, and highly segregated neighborhoods to form. Even a deliberately arranged viable pattern, as in Figure 3, when buffeted by a little random motion, proves unstable and gives way to the separate neighborhoods of Figures 5 through 8. These then prove to be fairly immune to continued random turnover.

For those who deplore segregation, however, and especially for those who deplore more segregation than people were seeking when they collectively segregated themselves, there may be a note of hope. The underlying motivation can be far less extreme than the observable patterns of separation. What it takes to keep things from unraveling is to be learned from Figure 4; the later figures indicate only how hard it may be to restore such "integration" as would satisfy the individuals, once the process of separation has stabilized. In Figure 4 only 9 of the 45 individuals are motivated to move, and if we could persuade them to stay everybody else would be all right. Indeed, the reader might exercise his own ingenuity to discover how few individuals would need to be invited into Figure 4 from outside, or how few individuals would need to be relocated in Figure 4, to keep anybody from wanting to move. If two lonely #'s join a third lonely #, none of them is lonely anymore, but the first will not move to the second unless assured that the third will arrive, and without some concert or regulation, each will go join some larger cluster, perhaps abandoning some nearby lonely neighbor in the process and surely helping to outnumber the opposite color at their points of arrival.

The Bounded-Neighborhood Model

Turn now to a different model, and change the definition of "neighborhood." Instead of everyone's defining his neighborhood by reference to his own location, there is a common definition of the neighborhood and its boundaries. A person is either inside it or outside. Everyone is concerned about the color *ratio* within the neighborhood but not with the arrangement of colors within the neighborhood. "Residence" can therefore just as well be interpreted as membership or participation in a job, office, university, church, voting bloc, restaurant, or hospital.

In this model there is one particular area that everybody, black or white, prefers to its alternatives. He will live in it unless the percentage of residents of opposite color exceeds some limit. Each person, black or white, has his own limit. ("Tolerance," I shall occasionally call it.) If a person's limit is exceeded in this area he will go someplace else—a place, presumably, where his own color predominates or where color does not matter.

"Tolerance," it should be noticed, is a *comparative* measure. And it is specific to this location. Whites who appear, in this location, to be less tolerant of *blacks* than other whites may be merely more tolerant of the alternative *locations*.

Evidently the limiting ratios must be compatible for some blacks and some whites—as percentages they must add to at least 100—or no contented mixture of any whites and blacks is possible. Evidently, too, if nobody can tolerate extreme ratios, an area initially occupied by one color alone would remain so.

There may be some number among the other color that, if concerted entry were achieved, would remain; but, acting individually, nobody would be the first.

We can experiment with frequency distributions of "tolerance" to see what results they lead to. (We cannot discover realistic distributions, because they would depend on the area in question; and the area in our model has not been named.) What we can do is to look at the process by which the area becomes occupied, or remains occupied, by blacks or whites or a mixture of both, and look for some principles that relate outcomes to the tolerances, the initial occupancies, and the dynamics of movement.

We assume that all preferences go in the same direction: a person need not care, but if he does care his concern takes the form of an *upper limit* to the other color that can occur in this area without his choosing to go elsewhere. There is no lower limit: there are no minority-seeking individuals, nor any who will leave if the area is not suitably integrated. Absolute numbers do not matter, only ratios. There are no individual positions within the mix: nobody is near the center or near the boundary, nobody has a "next neighbor."

To study the dynamics we assume that people both leave and return. (This is restrictive: if the preference for this locality were due merely to the fact that some people were already here and the cost of leaving were high, that cost would not be recovered by returning.) People in the area move out if the ratio is not within their color limit; people outside move in if they see that it meets their demands.

Information is perfect: everybody knows the color ratio at the moment he makes his choice. But people do not know the intentions of others and do not project future turnover. We need, too, the somewhat plausible assumption that, of two whites dissatisfied with the ratio, the more dissatisfied leaves first—the one with the lesser tolerance. Then, the whites within the locality will always have higher tolerances than any whites outside, and similarly for blacks inside and outside. The least tolerant whites move out first, and the most tolerant move in first, and the same for blacks.

Our initial data are cumulative frequency distributions of "tolerance" of the members of each color group. We can experiment with various distributions, but for the initial experiment we use a straight line.

An Illustrative Distribution of "Tolerance"

For the whites, the horizontal axis measures the number of whites, the vertical axis the ratio of blacks to whites representing the upper limits of their tolerances. Take the total of whites to be 100. Suppose the median white will live with blacks in equal numbers, so that 50 among the 100 whites will abide a black-white ratio of 1:0 or greater. The most tolerant will accept a ratio of 2:1 (is willing to be in a one-third minority); and the least tolerant will not stay in the presence of any blacks. The cumulative distribution of tolerances for whites will then appear as in the top of Figure 9. It is a straight line from 2:0 on the vertical axis to the 100 whites on the horizontal axis who comprise the white population.

Suppose blacks have an identical distribution of tolerance for whites but the number of blacks is half the number of whites, 50.

There are at least some whites and some blacks who could contentedly coexist. Fifty of the whites would be willing to live with all the blacks, though not all 50 blacks would be willing to live with 50 whites. A mixture of 25 blacks and 25 whites could be content together. There are 10 blacks who could tolerate a ratio of 1:6 to 1, or 16 whites; and any 16 among the 80 or so whites who will tolerate a black-white ratio of 10:16 would be content to join them. To explore all the combinations that might form a contented mix, but especially to study the dynamics of entry and departure, it is useful to translate both our schedules from ratios to absolute numbers, and to put them on the same diagram.

Translation of the Schedules

This is done in the bottom of Figure 9. The curve labeled
W is a translation of the white tolerance schedule. For each
number of whites along the horizontal axis the number of
blacks whose presence they will tolerate is equal to their own
number times the corresponding ratio on the schedule of tolerance. Thus 50 whites can tolerate an equal number of blacks,
or 50. Seventy-five can tolerate half their number, or 37.5; 25
can tolerate 1.5 times their number, or 37.5. Ninety can tolerate one-fifth of their number, or 18; 20 can tolerate 32, and so
forth.

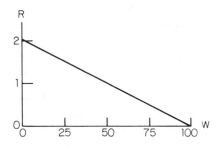

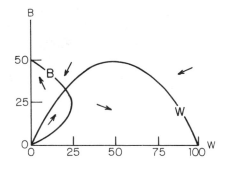

Figure 9

In this fashion the straight-line tolerance schedule translates into a parabolic curve showing the absolute numbers that correspond to the limits of tolerance of alternative numbers of whites. (Economists will recognize that the cumulative frequency distribution translates into this absolute-numbers curve in the same way that a demand curve translates into a total-revenue curve.) Similar arithmetic converts the blacks' schedule of tolerance into the smaller parabolic dish that opens toward the vertical axis in Figure 9.

Any point in Figure 9 that lies within the area of overlap denotes a combination of blacks and whites that can coexist. There are that many whites who will abide the presence of that many blacks, and there are that many blacks who will abide the presence of that many whites. Any point on the diagram that is beneath the whites' curve but to the right of the blacks' curve represents a mixture of whites and blacks such that all the whites are contented but not all the blacks. (Some of the blacks are content, but not all present.) And a point on the diagram that lies outside both curves—the region to the upper right—denotes a mixture of whites and blacks at which neither all the whites nor all the blacks could be satisfied; some of both colors would be dissatisfied.

Dynamics of Movement

It is the dynamics of motion, though, that determine what color mix will ultimately occupy the area. The simplest dynamics are as follows: if all whites in the area are content, and some outside would be content if they were inside, the former stay and the latter enter; whites continue to enter as long as all present are content, and some outside would be content if present. If not all whites present are content, some will leave; they will leave in order of their discontent, so that those remaining are the most tolerant; when their number in relation to the number of blacks is such that the whites remaining are all content, no more of them leave. A similar rule governs entry and departure of blacks.

We can now plot, for every point on the diagram, the directions of population change within this area. Within the overlapping portion of the two curves, the numbers of blacks and whites present will both be increasing. Within the white curve but outside the black curve, whites will be coming into the area and blacks departing; the direction of motion on the diagram will be toward the lower right, and nothing stops that motion until all blacks have departed and all whites have come in. To the upper left, within the black curve but beyond the white curve, blacks will be entering and whites departing; and the process can terminate only when all the whites have left and all the blacks have come in. Mixtures denoted by points outside both curves, to the upper right, will be characterized by the departure of both colors; when this movement brings one of the colors within its own curve, continued departure of the other color will improve the ratio for the color within its own curve; those who left will begin to return, and the other color will evacuate completely.

With the tolerance distributions of Figure 9, there are only two stable equilibria. One consists of all the blacks and no whites, the other all the whites and no blacks. Which of the two will occur depends on where the process starts and, perhaps, the relative speeds of white and black movement. If initially one color predominates it will move toward complete occupancy. If initially some of both are present, in "satisfied" numbers, relative speeds of black and white entry will determine which of the two eventually turns discontent and evacuates. If both are initially present in large numbers, relative speeds of exit will determine which eventually becomes content with the ratio, reverses movement, and occupies the territory.

There are, then, compatible mixes of the two colors—any mixture denoted by the overlap of the two curves. The difficulty is that any such mixture attracts outsiders, more of one color or both colors, eventually more of just one color, so that one color begins to dominate numerically. A few individuals of the opposite color then leave; as they do, they further reduce the numerical status of those of their own color who stay behind. A few more are dissatisfied, and they leave; the minority becomes even smaller, and cumulatively the process causes evacuation of them all.

Alternative Schedules

This, of course, is not the only possible result. The outcome depends on the shapes we attribute to the tolerance schedules and to the sizes of the white-black populations. The result we just reached does not depend on the fewness of blacks relative to whites: make the blacks' curve the same size as the whites' and the result is still a one-color equilibrium. But with steeper straightline schedules and equal numbers of blacks and whites, we can produce a stable mixture with a large number of blacks and whites.

Specifically, suppose that the median white can tolerate a ratio of 2.5 blacks per white, i.e., will inhabit this area even if whites are a minority of approximately 30 percent. Suppose the most tolerant can accept five to one and the least tolerant will not stay with any blacks. The tolerance schedule is a straight line with a vertical intercept at 5.0. If the blacks are equal in number and have an identical distribution of tolerance, the two schedules will translate into identical parabolas as shown in Figure 10.

Here, in addition to the two stable equilibria at 100 blacks and no whites and at 100 whites and no blacks, there is a stable mixture at 80 blacks and 80 whites. In fact, over a wide range of initial occupancies it is this mixed equilibrium that will be approached through the movement of blacks and whites. As long as half or more of both colors are present—actually, slightly over 40 percent of both colors—the dynamics of entry and departure will lead to the stable mixture of 80 blacks

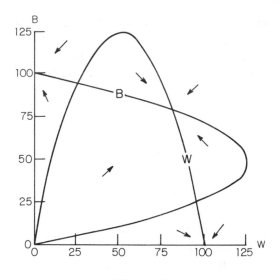

Figure 10

and 80 whites. Even for very small numbers of both colors present, if the initial ratios are within the slopes of the two curves (which allow somewhat more than four to one of either color) and if neither color tends to enter much more rapidly than the other, the two colors will converge on the 80–80 mixture. Still, if the area were initially occupied by either color, it would require the concerted entry of more than 25 percent of the other color to lead to this stable mixture. Thus each of the three equilibria—the all-white, the all-black, and the 80–80 mixture—is stable against fairly large perturbations.

Alternative Numbers

The mixed stable equilibrium generated in Figure 10 disappears if blacks exceed whites or whites exceed blacks by, say, two to one. In that case, one curve lies within the other curve, rather than intersecting it, as shown in Figure 11.

Restricting entry can sometimes produce a stable mixture. If the whites in the area are limited to 40 and if the most toler-

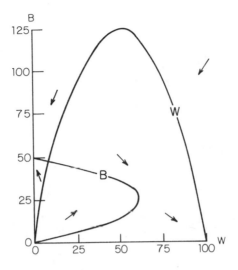

Figure 11

ant 40 are always the first to enter and the last to leave, the curves of Figure 11 are replaced by those of Figure 12, with a stable mixture at 40 whites and a comparable number of blacks. With the curves of Figure 9, however, both colors would have to be limited to yield a stable mixture.

Notice that limiting the number of whites has the same effect as if the whites in excess of that number had no tolerance at all. Whether they are excluded, or exclude themselves, it is their *absence* that keeps the whites from overwhelming the blacks by their numbers, and makes the stable mixture possible.

Thus it is not the case that "greater tolerance" always increases the likelihood of a stable mixture—not if "greater tolerance" means only that within a given population some members are statistically replaced by others more tolerant. On the contrary, replacing the two-thirds least tolerant whites in Figure 11 by even less tolerant whites keeps the whites from overwhelming the blacks by their numbers. (This would not happen if we made *all* whites less tolerant.)

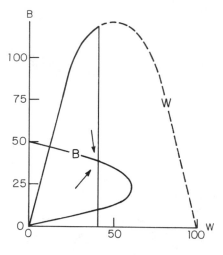

Figure 12

Varieties of Results

Evidently there is a wide variety of shapes of tolerance schedules that we could experiment with, and different ratios of blacks and whites. There is no room here for a large number of combinations, but the method is easy and the reader can pursue by himself the cases that most interest him. (The only logical restriction on the shape of the absolute-numbers curves is that a straight line from the origin intersect such a curve only once.)

Integrationist Preferences

Surprisingly, the results generated by this analysis do not depend upon each color's having a preference for living separately. They do not even depend on a preference for being in the majority!

For easy exposition it has been supposed that each person is limited in his "tolerance" for the other color and will go elsewhere if the ratio becomes too extreme. The question now arises, suppose these blacks and whites actually prefer mixed neighborhoods: what must we do to capture this neighborhood preference in a model of the sort already developed?

On reflection it appears that the analysis is already done. The same model represents both hypotheses. More than that, the same results flow from the two alternative hypotheses.

We postulate a preference for mixed living and simply reinterpret the same schedules of tolerance to denote the upper limits to the ratios at which people's preference for integrated residence is outweighed by their extreme minority status (or by their inadequate-majority status).

The same model fits both interpretations. The results are as pertinent to the study of preferences for integration as to the study of preferences for separation. (The only asymmetry is that we did not postulate a lower limit to the acceptable proportion of opposite color, i.e., an upper limit to the proportion of like color in the neighborhood.)

Policies and Instruments

The analysis is pertinent to the study of the way that numerical or ratio quotas or limits on numbers may affect the likelihood of a mixed stable equilibrium. It is equally pertinent to the study of concerted action. The occurrence of an intersection of the two curves that could constitute a stable equilibrium does not usually guarantee that that equilibrium will result. It usually competes with extreme mono-colored stable equilibria. When there are two or more potential stable equilibria, initial occupancies and rates of movement determine which one will result.

Getting "over the hump" from one stable equilibrium to another often requires either a large perturbation or concerted action. Acting in concert, people can achieve an alternative equilibrium. (Blacks and whites cannot both successfully concert in opposition to each other; either color, by concerted action, may overwhelm the other, but not both simultaneously.)

The model as described is limited in the phenomena it can handle because it makes no allowance for speculative behavior, for time lags in behavior, for organized action, or for misperception. It also involves a single area rather than many areas simultaneously affected. But it can be built on to accommodate some of those enrichments.[9]

[9] The analysis is pursued at greater length and in greater variety in Schelling, "Dynamic Models of Segregation," *Journal of Mathematical Sociology*, 1 (1971), 143–86.

5

SORTING AND MIXING:
AGE AND INCOME

CONSIDER AN ORGANIZATION whose members vary in age and care how old their associates are. To be concrete, suppose the age distribution is even from 20 to 70 and nobody will remain in a group whose average age exceeds his own by more than ten years or is less by more than twenty. Initially, with an even spread from 20 to 70, the mean is 45 and everybody under 35 will depart. So will everybody over 65. What happens to the group—the size of its membership and its age distribution?

Again what we have is people responding to an environment that consists of people who are responding to each other. As people respond they change the environments of the people they associate with, and cause further responses. Everybody's presence affects, if only slightly, the environment of everybody else. "Respond" in these cases is departure or, if we permit it, joining or rejoining. The outcomes are described in aggregates, averages, and frequency distributions. But the outcomes result from *individual* decisions, unless people can commit themselves to organized or disciplined choices.

Models of Sorting and Mixing

These are idealized models of sorting and mixing, or segregating and integrating. We postulate a population of individuals who respond to some specified characteristics of the population itself—some ratio or average or percentage of the total. We impute to the individuals certain preferences about those population characteristics, and we specify the dynamics of response.

Our interest in these models would arise from two conditions that may or may not hold. The first is that we be able to identify a model with some important social process, even if it

is only a remote and abstract model that captures part of the
process. The second is that the result not be trivial—that the
outcomes not be so transparently related to the parameters of
the model that we can proceed from postulates to results without working the model.

Discrete and Continuous Variables

This chapter is about models in which the variable to
which people respond is continuous. *Discrete* variables are
religion, language, sex, "color," nationality, political party, and
the dichotomous divisions between officers and enlisted men,
faculty and students, doctors and nurses. *Continuous* variables
are age, income, IQ, height, and skill at tennis or chess.
("Color" is in quotation marks because pigmentation is continuous in several dimensions, but for purposes of segregation
"color" is discrete and nearly dichotomous in this country.)
Some continuous variables, like age, are well defined and measurable. Some, like income, can be approximately defined, if
somewhat arbitrarily. Some, like IQ or skill at tennis, can be
ordered but not measured, and may or may not have been cali-
brated on a scale. Some, like "status," may involve too many
dimensions to be treated as a single variable even in an abstract
model.

Discrete and Continuous Actions

In addition to the population characteristics, the model has
to identify the activity. If we talk about segregation by race or
by age in residential neighborhoods, we need definitions not
only of "race" or "age" but of "residence" and "neighborhood."
We can work with a model in which my neighbor's neighborhood is the same as mine, a "bounded-neighborhood" model,
or one in which my neighbor's neighborhood extends a little
further in his direction and is different from mine but spatially
continuous with it. Thus the "environment" can also be contin-

uous or discrete. And the activity—association, contact, or even residence—can be an on-off variable or a continuous variable measured in proportions, frequencies, or distance.

The Constraining Identities

For the simplest example, consider an apartment house, nursing home, or neighborhood, and suppose no one is willing to stay where people on the average are older than oneself. The younger people move out; the average rises; somebody else is now younger than average and moves out; again the average rises and again somebody moves out. Eventually those who are tied for oldest are all that remain. The same would be true of a tennis club in which the poorest 10 percent of the players find membership unattractive.

What we have is a set of constraining "identities," mathematical conditions that cannot be evaded. For any variable by which people can be ranked or measured, in any group, half the members will be at or above the median. A quarter will be at or below the lower quartile; no more than 10 percent can be above the highest decile. Nobody can join or leave without changing everybody else's position. If people above average leave, the average goes down; if they join, it goes up.

If we divide a population in two, the weighted average of the two groups has to equal the average for the population as a whole. And we cannot have the younger people in the group with the higher average, and the older in the group with the lower average, no matter how badly they all want it that way.

The question of whether a grouping is possible in which everybody is satisfied is pertinent to "open-ended" models—models in which people depart if their absolute requirements are not met. In a "closed model," people move only if things are better in the place they move to; we rank people according to some variable, say age, and ask how they will distribute themselves among two or more compartments—neighborhoods, organizations, or just "compartments."

The Open Model

Consider now the question posed at the beginning. Initially there is an even distribution of ages from 20 to 70, with a mean of 45. Everybody under 35 is dissatisfied and will leave, as will everybody above 65. The outcome depends on the dynamics; so we have to specify whether all the dissatisfied make simultaneous decisions to depart the same day and do depart; or, if they do not move simultaneously, whether the young move out faster than the old and whether the 20-year-olds, who are "more discontent," move out faster than the 30-year-olds, who are discontent by only five years rather than fifteen.

Let all the discontents move out at once. We are left with an age spread from 35 to 65 and a mean of 50. Now everybody under 40 wants to move; the departure of more young people than old has raised the average. What about the people over 65? Do we let them back in? If we don't, the ultimate outcome will be a residual population consisting of everybody in the age range from 45 to 65. If we readmit the people who left before the average rose, and who would not have left if they had waited, we shall end up with an age range from 50 to 70.

Quite different initial conditions lead to the same result. If only the age group from 20 to 40 is initially in the organization, and if non-members can join when the age distribution appeals to them, older people will join. The younger will defect, and stability is eventually achieved with the 50–70 age group alone. People aged 40 to 50 will have joined, causing younger people to depart, only to leave in their turn as their presence attracts older members whom they cannot abide.

If there had been a gap in the age distribution—nobody aged 40 to 50—none of the older outsiders would have joined the initial 20–40 age group. Thus the intermediate ages dispossess the younger and are in turn dispossessed by the people they attract!

If everybody over forty is excluded from membership, the forty- and fifty-year-olds can object. If the restriction is lifted they will join, only to quit as the sixty– and seventy–year–olds, who originally were uninterested, follow them in.

Closed Models

Imagine a group of people, differing in age, with a choice of two rooms—dining halls, perhaps. Everybody wants to be in the dining hall in which the average age is nearest his own. Is there an equilibrium? How is equilibrium arrived at, and how will the process be affected by rules of movement, errors of perception, the order in which different people make their choices and the speeds with which they act, and whether adjustment is continuous or there is a limited number of attempts?

Evidently we can find an equilibrium. Spread everybody in a line by age and make a partition. The marginal person, located at the partition, prefers the older group or the younger group or is indifferent. If he prefers the older group, put him into it by moving the partition, and keep doing that until the marginal individual no longer prefers the older group. At that first partition there was some number of people, say on the younger side, who preferred to be on the older side; as we move individuals from the younger group to the older, we lower the average ages in both groups. Some who were originally content to be in the younger group will prefer to move into the older, as the higher average approaches their own age and the lower average moves away. But it is easily determined that we reach an equilibrium (even if it contains only the youngest person in one room). With a few plausible assumptions about the speed with which people move and the speed with which they can estimate that parameter (arithmetic mean, for example) in which they are interested, we can generate a damped adjustment process that will converge on a division of people into the two rooms. But there are other preferences to consider.

There is the extreme case in which everybody wants to be in the room with the highest average. A possible equilibrium is that everybody ends up in one room. (Whether or not this is actually an "equilibrium" will depend on whether we let the oldest person move into the empty room, attracted by the potential average when he alone is in it.)

Another possibility is that people who are above average want to be in the room with the lower average, and vice versa. There are more complicated preferences.

Alternative Preferences in Closed Models

An interesting family of preferences has the following properties. The "preferred mean age" is higher, the higher one's age, and mean ages are more preferred, the closer they are to the preferred mean. This simplified family of preferences focuses only on the arithmetic mean; and it is by no means evident that a single statistic, like a population mean, is all that people would care about. But as a warming-up exercise, it is instructive.

Let me illustrate, with as simple an example as can be created, the kinds of questions that arise and some of the answers one can get. I shall refer to "age," but at this level of abstraction any other measure would do. (Because the example uses the arithmetic mean as the motivating statistic, a measureable quantity is implied. But with an even distribution the mean coincides with the median.)

Imagine a population evenly distributed between the ages of 0 and 100. There are two rooms—again, two dining halls on the same floor can be our image—and everybody is free to enter the room of his choice and to change to the other room if it has the mean age that he prefers. Nobody cares about the rooms themselves; everybody cares about the ages of the people he is with. We can try some alternative preference structures.

1. Everybody prefers the room in which the average age is closest to his own.
2. Everybody prefers a room in which the average age is a little higher than his own. Specifically, everybody prefers an average age that exceeds his own by a fraction of the

difference between his own age and the highest age, 100; and that fraction is the same for everybody, whatever his age. (If the fraction is one-third, a 40-year-old prefers the room whose average age is nearest to 60.)

3. Everybody prefers the group whose average age is a little closer than his own to the population average of 50. Specifically, everybody prefers a mean age closer to 50 by some uniform fraction of the difference. (If the fraction is one-fifth, a 30-year-old wants the room whose mean age is closest to 34.)

A little reflection suggests that any stable partition has to be by age, everybody above a certain age in one room, everybody below in the other. Then the first preference is easily handled: if everybody wants the room whose mean age is nearest his own there is a stable equilibrium at fifty-fifty. With a split at year 40, the mean age in one room is 20 and in the other, 70; everybody 40 to 45 would move into the younger group, raising the average in both rooms—to 22.5 and 72.5—so that everybody 45 to 47.5 wants to move into the younger group, and so on until the division is at 50 years.

The second set of preferences is more complicated. Everyone wants the room whose mean age is nearest to an age that is higher than his own by a fraction of the difference between his own and 100. If everyone wants to be with a group whose mean age is older than himself by one-third of that difference, the 25-year-old will want to be in the room whose mean age is nearest 50. With a split at age 50, the means in the two rooms will be 25 and 75; and the 25-year-old is indifferent. The 30-year-old is not. He prefers the mean age closest to 53. Everybody over 25 moves into the older room, lowering the mean age in both rooms, and the process unravels until everybody is in the same room. (When it gets down to the newborns they prefer the room with everybody, mean age 50, to a room of their own, mean age zero, 33 being their preferred mean.)

A little algebra shows that unless that fraction—the parameter in our preference formula—is less than .25 there is no sustainable division into two rooms. If that fraction is less than .25, there is a sustainable division at the age given by

100 $(1–4a)/(2–4a)$ where a is that fraction. If the fraction is .2, the stable division occurs at age 16.7; if .1, the stable division is at 37.5. And of course if the fraction is 0, the formula gives us our fifty-fifty split.

This is an example of "equilibrium analysis." The algebra is elementary. To work up to it we can ask what numerical value of that fraction would sustain a division at, say, age 30. A division into two rooms is sustainable only if the youngest person in the older room and the oldest person in the younger room are both satisfied. With division at age 30, the mean age in the younger group is 15 and in the older group 65; midway between is 40. If a 30-year-old prefers a mean age above 40 he will move to the older room; if he prefers it below 40 he'll move to the younger; and if 40 is the mean age he prefers, he is indifferent. So division at 30 is stable only if 30-year-olds prefer 40—older than themselves by 10/70 of the difference between their age and 100.

Division at zero would require that newborns be indifferent between mean ages of zero and 50; they must prefer 25, and the largest fraction that will sustain a division is therefore one-quarter.

To find the formula we stipulate algebraically that the person whose age is the dividing age prefer a mean halfway between the means of the two groups. If division occurs at age D, the mean in the younger room will be $D/2$; and in the older room, $(100 + D)/2$; the midpoint between them is half their sum, $[D/2 + (100 + D)/2]/2$, or $25 + D/2$. The person of age D prefers a mean age that exceeds D by a times $(100–D)$. His preferred mean coincides with the midpoint of the two means, then, if

$$D + a(100 - D) = D/2 + 25$$
$$D - aD - D/2 = 25 - 100a$$
$$D[1/2 - a] = 100[1/4 - a]$$
$$D = 100 \left[\frac{(1 - 4a)/4}{(1 - 2a)/2} \right]$$
$$= 100(1 - 4a)/(2 - 4a)$$

The third preference, in which everybody prefers a group mean closer than his own age to the population mean, allows three possibilities. If the fraction of the distance from his own age to the population mean that he prefers is greater than .5, no split will be sustained. Everybody will be in the same room. If the fraction is less than .5, an even split is stable. And if the fraction exactly equals .5, any division by age is in neutral equilibrium.

This is one of those results that are not obvious beforehand but quickly become transparent. Notice that for any dividing age, the midpoint between the two group means coincides with the midpoint between 50 and the dividing age. $[25 + D/2] = (50 + D)/2$. For example, dividing the population at age 60 we have two groups with mean ages 30 and 80, midpoint 55, which is exactly halfway between 50 and 60.

With division at age 50, nobody is motivated to move; the 50-year-olds are indifferent and everybody else prefers the mean on his own side of 50, 75 if he is over 50, 25 if he is under. But for division at, say, age 60, one of three things happens.

One is that everybody prefers a mean closer to his own age than to 50. In that case people at and near the dividing age prefer the mean age of the older group. Division at age 60 causes people around 60 to prefer the mean closest to an age greater than 55, so they join the smaller, older group, making it larger. People at the dividing age always prefer the smaller group's mean, and migration occurs until the division is at age 50.

The second is that everybody prefers a mean between his own age and 50, but closer to 50. In that case, for any division other than exactly age 50, people around the dividing age prefer the larger group's mean age. At age 60, they prefer a mean that is less than 55, which is closer to 30 than to 80. So they move, and are followed in turn by everybody else in that smaller, older group, because the marginal people—people near the dividing age—always prefer the younger mean of the larger group. (The centenarians prefer joining everybody else, mean age 50, to staying in their own 100-year-old group.)

The dividing line between these two opposite movements is a preference for a mean age exactly halfway between one's own and 50. In that special case the people at the dividing line are always indifferent between the two means because their preferred mean is the midpoint between the two. Any division is then an example of what is called a "neutral equilibrium."

Notice another special possibility. If people prefer the mean closer to 50 than their own age, but the actual division is at exactly age 50, nobody will move. There is no "larger" group whose mean is preferred by people at the dividing age. But if the people from 48 to 52 happen all to get into the same room, and the means go to 24 and 74, the alert 47-year-old will move to where the 48-year-olds are—the larger, older group—because he prefers a mean closer to 74. The 47-year-olds will be followed by the 46-year-olds. So while division at 50 in this case is an "equilibrium"—nobody motivated to move unless somebody else does first—it is an *unstable equilibrium*. Any departure is not self-correcting but self-aggravating, leading to larger and larger departure from the original unstable equilibrium. The new, stable equilibrium is all in one room. This one is "stable" because any departures from it will be reversed.

A Slightly More General Formula

Keeping the horizontal distribution, which is algebraically convenient, we can examine what happens if we use some other statistic than the arithmetic mean. The mean and the median coincide, but we can ask what happens if people want to be in the group whose lower or upper quartile, or fourth or sixth decile, is closest to some preferred value—the preferred value again being their own ages or some regular displacement from their own ages.

Our first preference is easily transposed into quartile or decile terms. Suppose everybody wants to be in the group whose age at the lowest quartile is nearest his own. With a horizontal distribution we can work this one in our heads. The division will occur where the marginal person—the oldest person in the younger group, and the youngest person in the older group—is equidistant in age between the lower quartiles of the two groups. Because of our even distribution, this means that three quartiles in the younger group cover the same age span as one quartile in the older group. The older group therefore spans three times the years of the younger group. So the division occurs at the lower quartile of the whole population, with one-third as many people in the younger room as in the older room.

The result generalizes (still for horizontal distribution): for any "fractile" that people want closest to their own ages, one-tenth or two-fifths or three-quarters, the equilibrium division into two rooms occurs at that fractile. The even split we obtained when we used the arithmetic means was due to the coincidence of the mean with the median, which divides the population at one-half.

A single formula takes care of these alternatives. Let everybody prefer the group whose P'th percentile is closest to the age that lies some fraction, a, of the distance from his own age to some reference age, R. If everybody wants the group whose lowest quartile is closest to one-fifth the distance from his own age, x, to age 60, then P is .25, a is .2, and R is 60; and he prefers the group whose 25th percentile is closest to $x + .2(60-x)$. If the population is divided at age D, D is a stable dividing point if and only if:

$$D + a(R - D) = \frac{PD + D + P(100 - D)}{2}$$

or, $$D = \frac{P - 2aR/100}{1 - 2a}100$$

Using $P = .5$ for the median (mean) as before, and $R = 100$ or 50 as before, we get $D = (1-4a)/(2-4a)$ and $D = \frac{1}{2}$ as before. The formula breaks down—there is no stable dividing point—if the numerator is negative; so when $P = .5$, the maximum values for a are .25 and .5 when R is equal to 100 and to 50.

The formula is not worth memorizing, since populations and preferences don't fit this idealized model. But for gaining familiarity with the way this kind of model works, the formula is suggestive.

A Third Room

If a third dining hall were available, would anybody occupy it? Just as the second room will be unoccupied if the value of a is large, the third will not be occupied unless a is quite small. We can suppose an equilibrium division into two rooms and ask whether the youngest person in the younger room would move to a third room if it were available, the mean or median age in that third room then being his own. With the horizontal distribution that we are using for arithmetical convenience, the mean age in the younger room will be half the age at which the population is divided. The youngest, whose age is zero, will move into a third room if his preferred mean age, aR, is closer to zero than to a mean equal to half the age that divides the two occupied rooms. That is, if:

$$4aR < \frac{P - 2aR/100}{1 - 2a}100$$

Using the mean (median) as the statistic of interest, $P = .5$, with R equal to 100, i.e., with everyone preferring a somewhat higher mean than his own age, the third room will form only if a is less than about .096. With R equal to 50, so that the reference age is the population mean, a third room will form with a less than .25.

With R equal to 100, the oldest member will always prefer to occupy the third room if it is empty. So with three rooms available, the population will settle down only if a is less than

.096; otherwise, the younger will move into upper age groups, vacating the youngest room, which then attracts the oldest again. With R equal to 50, and a less than .25, the vacant room will initially be occupied by the oldest or the youngest, whoever gets there first, but the end result will be the same.

Optimality of Division or Non-Division

Does the equilibrium division into two rooms represent some optimal, or welfare maximizing, or collectively preferred division? We should not expect so because nobody in our model pays any heed to what he does to the average age of any group he joins.

We can ask, for example, whether the equilibrium division minimizes the sum of the distances between actual mean ages and people's preferred mean ages. Satisfaction need not be proportionate to that distance; but it could be, and at least for illustration we can ask what happens to the sum of the differences between the mean ages people prefer and the mean ages they get.

With reference age R at 100, it turns out that for any positive value of a the aggregate difference is not minimized at the equilibrium division. Actually, the larger is a, the greater the disparity. Look for a moment at the situation when a is .25. Everybody congregates in a single room. What happens if we force the older half into one room and the younger half into another?

Everybody in the older room gains. People aged 50 have a preferred mean age of 62.5, which is midway between 50, the previous mean, and 75, the new one. In the younger room, the youngest third—the youngest sixth of the population—is better off. They prefer their new mean of 25 to the old mean of 50. The next sixth of the population, those from the 16.7th to the 33.3rd percentile, are worse off—they prefer 50 to 25—but they would not voluntarily move to the older room, because its mean is 75, and they prefer 25 to 75. The next sixth, from the

33.3rd percentile to the 50th, are worse off and would switch to the older group if they could, preferring a mean of 75 to 25. But if, for all of these people, we calculate the changes in the distances between their preferred means and the means of the groups they are in, we find that division into two rooms reduces that aggregate distance. In fact, the aggregate distance is minimized when they are divided with the older 40 percent in one room, the younger 60 percent in the other.[10]

This illustrates that an equilibrium division is not likely to have any optimal properties. And it reminds us that an imposed division will benefit some, will dissatisfy some who nevertheless would not switch voluntarily, and will leave some discontent who would switch if they could.

The Need for Models

I return to the two circumstances in which models like these are useful. First, they must be models of something that matters—residence or membership or participation that involves separation or mixing of some social significance. And second, the systemic consequences of individual behaviors must not be so transparent that we can treat the aggregate as though it were a collective individual, and do without the model.

I have been trying to demonstrate the second circumstance, in which the outcomes are not immediately and intuitively transparent even though the motivations have been postulated

---

[10] The accounting, with everybody over 60 in one room and under 60 in the other, compared with all in one room, is as follows. Everybody over 60 prefers the separation. Everybody 40 to 60 is in the younger room but would prefer the current mean age, 80, of the older room. (These are the people who would have to be induced to stay in the younger room.) Everybody 20 to 40 prefers the previous situation—one room with a mean age of 50—to the new, but would not be attracted to the older room with its current mean of 80. Everybody under 20 prefers the new mean of his room, 30, to the previous mean of 50. Sixty percent of the people gained, 40 percent lost; the mean displacement is 6.67 years closer (about one-third closer) to the mean of one's choice than it was with all in one room.

and the population characteristics specified. In such cases, studies of aggregates will not permit inferences about individual motives, without the help of a mediating model. And knowledge of individual behaviors will not by itself lead either to predictions of aggregate outcomes or to policies for affecting those outcomes. Attention must be paid to the macrophenomena that are the object of policy.

Simplified models of artificial stiuations can be offered for either of two purposes. One is ambitious: these are "basic models"—first approximations that can be elaborated to simulate with higher fidelity the real situations we want to examine. The second is modest: whether or not these models constitute a "starting set" on which better approximations can be built, they illustrate the *kind* of analysis that is needed, some of the phenomena to be anticipated, and some of the questions worth asking.

The second, more modest, accomplishment is my only aim in the preceding demonstrations. The models were selected for easy description, easy visualization, and easy algebraic treatment. But even these artificial models invite elaboration. In the closed model, for example, we could invoke a new variable, perhaps "density," and get a new division between the two rooms at a point where the greater attractiveness of the age level is balanced by the greater crowding. To do this requires interpreting "room" concretely rather than abstractly, with some physical dimension or some facility in short supply. (A child may prefer to be on the baseball squad which has older children, but not if he gets to play less frequently; a person may prefer to travel with an older group, but not if it reduces his chances of a window seat; a person may prefer the older discussion group, but not if it means a more crowded room, more noise, fewer turns at talking, and less chance of being elected chairman.) As we add dimensions to the model, and the model becomes more particular, we can be less confident that our model is of something we shall ever want to examine. And after a certain amount of heuristic experiments with building blocks, it becomes more productive to identify the actual characteristics of the phenomena we want to study, rather than to explore general properties of self-sorting on a continuous variable. Nursing homes, tennis clubs, bridge tournaments, social groupings, law firms, apartment buildings, undergraduate colleges, and dancing classes may display a number of similar phenomena in their membership; and there may be a number of respects in which age, I.Q., walking speed, driving speed, income, seniority, body size, and social distinction motivate similar behaviors. But the success of analysis eventually depends as much on identifying what is peculiar to one of them as on the insight developed by studying what is common to them.

Some Applications

An example that is easy to visualize, and not difficult to find, is residential homes for the elderly. These usually correspond to our "open model," a place that one can join or leave, although not without cost. (The open model can always be recognized as a special case of the closed model, with the rest of the world as the second alternative, but so large that its population characteristics are invariant with respect to the size of the membership.)

It is not feasible to compose a residential unit with elderly people of identical ages. Many are married couples. Vacancies occur irregularly through death and disability, and replacements have to be found. Markets are localized, and people seeking such housing are too few to provide stratified allocations into sizable buildings, while if the units are small they will cease to be the "units" that people identify as their environments. And age, for purposes of living together, is not strictly chronological but is a cluster of attributes, like vigor and diet and eyesight and memory, which vary at a given age and with time.

So there will be a mix of ages. And the question does arise:

Can there be found, among the interested population, a group of people with an age mix that every member of the group is willing to live with? As we have seen, there is no guarantee that such a group exists, even if the elderly prefer to live among the elderly. (The mathematics are like that of the freshmen class of an elite college: if nobody can bear to be in the bottom 10 percent, according to some common measure, and if everybody's percentile position is predictable, and if everybody gets to know the composition of the class before he commits himself, there will be no sustainable freshmen class.)

A related question: If people of a given age have different feelings about the groupings they are willing to live in, some willing to be youngest and others not, or some willing to be the oldest and others not, so that we can form groups that, say, all of the 80-year-olds will join but only some of the 60-year-olds, what fraction of the total elderly population can be attracted if the groupings are skillfully composed?

A third question: If with free entry and exit we cannot find viable groupings of any size, and if we can impose restrictions or inducements to lure people in or to induce them to stay out, will our problem be to bring people in or to keep people out? Or are they alternatives? (Keeping some of the old out may keep some of the young in.)

Still another question: If a group is not viable, how large is the fraction that needs to be induced to remain in order that the rest stay voluntarily? Remember the problem posed at the beginning of this chapter. We ended up with the people 50 to 70. If we add the people 40 to 50, the mean age drops from 60 to 55, and the group from 45 to 50 (which would not have joined on its own) will remain as long as the 40 to 45s can be induced to remain.

Age has an interesting characteristic: it changes in a regular way with the passage of time. So for any group or cohort we can ask the above questions on a time scale. If a group is viable now, will its age mix still suit its members in five years —ten years? If it is not, but we can hold it together for a while, will it become viable? If we find a viable group with the youngest at, say, 65 and perpetually replenish the group with 65-year-olds as older people die, does the age distribution generated by the mortality table represent a viable group?

Some Other "Sorting Variables"

Students probably have preferences about the scholarship levels and athletic proficiencies of the colleges they attend. Some people like to excel; they like to participate; they like to be stimulated; and they like the prestige of attending a quality college or playing on a quality team. The net effect may be to prefer a college that ranks, on average, a little above one's self. Admissions policies hold down the population density of the higher ranked colleges; and if aptitude is the currency with which one buys admission, people will be stratified among colleges according to these ranking variables. (This could be incidental to the quality of the faculty and the facilities.)

The Structure of the Model

The simplest among these models can be described as follows. There is some population statistic to which each person relates in two ways. The person has a *preference* about that statistic, and the person *contributes* something to that statistic. These two relations are usually distinct: being middle-aged is different from liking to associate with middle-aged people, being rich is different from liking to associate with rich people. But the two relations, though distinct, are correlated.

Without correlation, people who congregated out of a common preference would be just a sample of the population, with nothing to congregate about (except preference). If preferences and contributions are negatively correlated, there will be a tendency toward regression. Any cluster of people who together produce a local population statistic away from the average, toward either extreme, will seek to join another group toward the opposite extreme, which in turn will be full of individuals seeking company like the first group. If the fat want to associate with the lean and the lean with the fat, separate lean and fat groupings will not survive.

It is when there is positive correlation between the preferred values and the contributed values that separation can occur.

There is one statistic to which everyone contributes equally but about which their preferences may differ. That is population size, or density. Some like crowded beaches and coffeehouses, others like solitude. Leaving out body size, everybody contributes 1.0 to the statistic of his group. With no variation there is no correlation, so the correlation principle expressed above is no help; but again let there be two rooms.

If everybody wants the less crowded dining hall, stability will occur with equal densities; if everybody wants the more crowded room, all will be in it. If the two rooms are equal in size and all want to be in the room that more nearly contains 55 percent of the total, all will be in one room! (Forcibly separating anything over 10 percent into the other room will make everybody better off: 15 is closer to 55 than 100 is. But they won't stay there on their own because 85 is still closer.)

If people differ in the densitites they prefer, the division between two rooms is governed by whoever prefers a density of exactly half the total number. (With rooms of equal size, densities are proportionate to numbers; the midpoint between the two numbers is equal to half the total.) If fewer than half the people want to be in a room with more than half, people will divide equally. If more than half want to be with more than half, they will divide where the marginal person prefers a room with just half. If among 100 people the preferences are evenly distributed from, say, 20 per room to 120 per room, then 30 people prefer a room with less than 50, 70 prefer a room with more than 50, and they will divide with densities of 30 and 70. And any other distribution of preferences with the thirtieth person just preferring 50 in his room will also cause the same 30:70 division.

Market Analogies

In some cases people genuinely care about their associates
—about their age or income or I.Q. But there are market phenomena which operate on an impersonal level and still have
many of the characteristics of these segregation models.

Consider an insurance scheme in which everybody pays the
same premium and those who die or experience injury are
compensated, or their beneficiaries are. The people who are
least likely to die or to hurt themselves get the poorest bargain.
If they know it, and if the organization is unable to discriminate in its premiums, they will leave to form an association of
their own—one that charges lower premiums to those who can
identify themselves as low risks and that excludes the higher
risks. As they leave, they raise the mortality and accident rates
in the organization that they leave, and the premiums have to
go up. More people leave. If everybody whose expected value
is negative departs, there will be nobody left. (If everybody is
willing to pay a fee for insurance, the scheme may unravel
until what remains is an extremely high-mortality, high-acci-
dent group that is small enough to have a mean rate of compensation that is within the fee limit of the least-benefited
member. But if the distribution is exponential, there is no such
group.) If institutionally the groups cannot discriminate in
their premiums among members but can exclude higher risks
from membership, members will get sorted into different groups
according to their mortality and accident classes. In this case it
is not the people themselves that one cares about, but the costs
they inflict by being added into the numerator of one's own
group.[11]

In the same way a dining hall that charges a flat price,
which just covers costs, is a bargain for people who like the

[11] An excellent and original discussion of market phenomena of this
type is George A. Akerlof's, "The Market for 'Lemons,' " 488–500. [see
note 6.]

expensive dishes or large helpings; the salad-bar crowd will be paying more than it's worth. If they drop out the price has to go up, now the people who eat meat, but not much, are helping to pay for the football team's diet, and they too may leave to find an economical alternative. Eventually, only the expensive eaters are left, and even they may now be paying more than they can afford! In the end, they may depart in search of more modest fare at a price closer to what they were originally paying. There goes the dining hall.

The fact that many homes for the elderly have an annuity feature or large initiation fee, and many services are available at no cost because discrimination is offensive, adds this market dimension to the situation of the elderly.

Change with the Passage of Time

What happens to the variable associated with an individual as time goes by? Age is special: age goes up by a year every year. And it does so independently of the ages of the people who surround one. In the earlier years of life, the age spread that one can tolerate probably widens with the passage of time. So if the age distribution in some group is not stable but can be made to wait a while, mutual compatibility may develop.

A person who plays bridge or tennis improves at a rate that depends to a large extent upon the skill of the people in his club. Likely there is some optimum differential between the mean skill that surrounds a person and his own skill. Then a fixed contingent of people may develop a reduced dispersion of skill over time, the better players not improving so much for lack of competition, the poorest dropping out because they can't stand the competition, and the rest showing improvement in proportion to the difference between each one's own skill and the mean skill (or some other statistic) of the group.

Status may be the same: in academic or other life, one acquires status from associating with people of status. And just as this can be part of the motive for associating, it can diminish the dispersion of status in a group, as individuals gradually become assimilated into the status of the group.

Mediating Variables

I have been supposing that people of different ages, incomes, or I.Q.'s care about the ages, incomes, or I.Q.'s of the people they associate with. But the preferences are often about something that is a function of age, income, I.Q., or skill. Among children, size and strength and age and skill are so closely associated that, when children sort themselves by age, as in baseball, the operative variables may be strength and skill. The school system sorts children by age but it can do so because age is associated with size, strength, skill, experience, and prior schooling. Adults may sort themselves by age because of family status and because of lifestyle. People of an age to have children want to live where life is adapted to children, i.e., to families in which the parents are mostly of similar age.

People who like privacy will associate with people who like privacy, not necessarily because they like the people but because they like the privacy. People who dislike dogs are happier among people who dislike dogs, not because they like the people but because there are no dogs. People who like crowds will be crowded with people who like crowds, without necessarily liking the people who like crowds. People who want to participate in a life-annuity scheme want to participate with short-lived people, without particularly preferring to have friends who are not long for this world.

6

CHOOSING OUR CHILDREN'S GENES

"**C**HOOSING OUR CHILDREN'S GENES" has several interpretations. Usually it means all of us, collectively, choosing the genes of the next generation. They are all "our children," whether or not we are actually parents. If the title referred to traditional eugenics, it would actually mean the process of choosing our children's *parents*.

Here I intend a literal interpretation. I am going to talk about each of us choosing *our own* children's genes, not determining genetic policy for other people and their children.

I am furthermore going to discuss choosing genes for children who are literally and biologically *our* children—not choosing genes from a donor, or a manufacturer. If my wife and I, or your husband and you, could choose from the available genetic menu a particular inheritance—for me of my child, for you of your child—what choices might we make? What difference might it make?

The Menu of Choice

When two people get together to have a child the number of genetically different children they could have is a large one. The particular child they have is randomly selected, according to current theory, from among a number of potential children that is more than ten thousand times the population of the earth. That is about how many chromosomally different children a single couple could have.

There are about eight million (2^{23}) genetically distinct sperm that a husband can produce and eight million distinct eggs that a wife might have produced, although she does not produce anything like that number of eggs. If you multiply those numbers together, you get the number of potentially different children, any one of which the couple might have conceived. I am going to explore some of the issues that would arise if a couple could exercise some choice among those sixty trillion genetically different children.

Despite the large number, this choice is narrowly limited. For me it is limited to the chromosomes that my wife and I possess. We probably cannot have a child as tall as Kareem Jabbar or as musical as Bach, or even a child that looks much like someone who reads this book. We are limited to a number of twofold choices from a limited packet of information that I contain, and an even more limited number of messages that my wife contains. So while there are more than sixty trillion possible different children we might have, the actual number to select them from may be only a few tens of millions. And, like it or not, most of them are going to look like my wife and me. They are not going to depart radically from the types of people that our parents, grandparents, and great-grandparents were.

Notice that within this choice every child is a natural child. Any child that we might select by intervening in the process of choosing our chromosomes—eliminating the lottery and making it a matter of choice—is a child whose likelihood of being born to us at random is the same as for every other potential child we might have had. There is nothing artificial, nothing manufactured. There is no reason, except improbability, why any child that we might choose couldn't be the child we would have had.

Among the eight million or so genetically distinct sperm that a father can produce, not only do they all resemble his own inheritance but the inheritance comes in a limited number of packages (twenty-three). (I am supposing that we cannot break open the chromosomes and select genes, but are limited to whole chromosomes.) If it turns out that you get not only the musical talent of a paternal grandmother but also her bad eyesight, you have to make a choice. If the traits are in the same package, you cannot pick and choose gene by gene; only chromosome by chromosome.

The Technology of Selection

I shall skip—and some of you will think I am cheating—the technology of how this may someday be done. To state it briefly, one has to identify *which* chromosome of the two, among any one of the pairs we are interested in, a fetus has, or a sperm or an egg possesses. One then has to identify the characteristics that are determined by that chromosome. (That may not be directly observable.) The characteristics then may have to be traced through the ancestors of the individual. And then there has to be a selection or rejection. The object of selection would be either fetus or sperm. (If it should be possible to screen sperm and eggs, there would be a very limited selection of eggs, depending on how many the technology makes available at any time for examination and activation, and a large variety of sperm; the choice would then be exercised much more on the male side of the family than on the female side.)

The energy required to examine a single cell and to determine which chromosome it contains may be enough energy to threaten the cell; there would then be no safe way to screen sperm and eggs, only fetuses.[12] That means a *very* limited choice. One will not search among millions of sperm, but look at one fetus at a time and decide whether it is worthwhile to stop and try again.

Whether or not it will appear worthwhile will likely depend on whether people are limited to taking cellular material from the amniotic fluid that surrounds the fetus, which may not be safe before about three months, or instead will have techniques for obtaining fetal cellular material earlier in pregnancy without harming the fetus.

One example we have—to prove that this is not an empty

---

[12] Except for chromosomes that determine sex, which affect the size and weight and even the mortality of the sperm and might allow separation by centrifugation or other separative techniques.

category of choice—is that it is now medically feasible to ascertain the sex of a fetus and to abort it if the parents don't want that sex. There are other chromosomal characteristics that can be identified; those that receive most attention at present are related to some pathology.

At present it is a costly choice at best. The fetus must be carried for about three months, preferably without a close sense of parental identification so that a choice could actually be made to discard it and start over. Starting over, one loses a likely minimum of six months between pregnancies; and it surely costs anxiety and loss of enjoyment of the early months of pregnancy, enjoyment both for parents and possible siblings. So it is by no means inexpensive to abort and start over. But it can be done.

If it turns out that cellular material can be obtained and a diagnosis performed within a week or two of conception, the choice may become nearly costless—just a matter of which month one decides to let oneself become pregnant according to the sex or other selected characteristics of the potential child.

Peculiarities of the Sex Choice

Choice of sex is different from most other choices. People are presently at liberty to express wishes for a boy or a girl. It may be hard for a wife to talk about whether she would not like somebody quite as short as her husband, and whether she wished her own musical talent rather than her husband's lack of it to be inherited in the children. They may find it difficult to discuss whether any ethnic characteristics that she or her husband has would look nice in a boy or a girl. But it is not improper to discuss—indeed it is hard to avoid some discussing —whether they would like to have a boy or a girl. So there is a legitimacy to that choice that other choices may not yet have. (The legitimacy may be dependent on the belief that there is no real choice—that no decision is at stake—and it is all idle conversation!)

But because *that* choice is feasible, it may induce the kind of technology—it may cover, so to speak, the social overhead costs of developing the technology—by which one can begin to select for chromosomes other than the one that determines the sex of the child.

There may also come with choosing the sex of children some experience, both demographic and intrafamilial experience, with what happens when people intervene in what used to be God's choice, or used to be a choice that God left to chance.

It is probably important, too, that many characteristics that people might choose for their children depend on the sex of the child. An example is body size. My impression is that many people would deplore a boy that is too small but would not so much deplore a girl who is small, and might equally deplore a girl that is "too large" but not so a boy. Inasmuch, therefore, as many of the things that people might choose, if they could choose, would depend on the sex of the child, the sex choice is in many ways an important entry into the subject.

Choosing the Sex of Children

Imagine that it were possible to choose in advance the sex of children. It is an easy idea to toy with; there is no difficulty in knowing what it means.

We can already choose whether to have children at all, at what age to have them, how many to have and how to space them over time; we can even somewhat control the sex composition by, for example, stopping when we already have a boy and a girl or trying again if we don't yet have what we want. Exercising a choice of sex would not lead to any new kinds of families: all the family combinations of boys and girls already exist.

Our interest is in the consequences, not the technology, and in how we deal with a choice that has never mattered before. But the technology itself can affect some of the questions we want to pursue. For example, is the technology under the control of the mother alone or does it require cooperation between the parents; will it be known whether or not the choice was exercised and to whom will it be known; and if a girl is decided on and a boy is born is it likely due only to the imperfect reliability of the method, or due to carelessness, or due to cheating? If a child ever wonders whether he or she was "wanted," the advent of contraception can affect the child's acceptance of a positive answer; will the technology of sex choice be such that the child will know what sex its parents tried for, and how likely it is they succeeded?

Leaving those questions behind, let's speculate on how people would choose if they did choose. Speculate is all we can do. There is no real evidence. We cannot investigate what people do in fact choose, because they do not in fact choose. And even if we ask them, as several researchers have done from time to time, it is hard to take the responses very seriously.

It is a little like the question, what would you ask for if you caught an enchanted sturgeon and were offered three wishes to let it go free? Not expecting the opportunity, you are unlikely to spend much time making plans for it. The sex of children is a question about which most people—not everybody but most people—are unprepared, especially people who have not yet had their first child. Nobody would dream of making a decision within the short time the interviewer will wait for an answer; and no couple is going to attempt to reconcile any differences they have, or even delicately explore each other's preferences, for the sake of providing a hypothetical statistic in a survey.

There have been attempts, now that contraception has been widespread and additions to American families can be interpreted as partly intentional, to look at any sex preferences that may be revealed in actual choices of whether or not to go on and have another child. The idea is simple: if families with two girls or two boys more frequently have a third child than families with one of each, this could mean that people want at least one of each and keep trying if they don't get them in the first two. But the statistics don't show much, and there are other interpretations. It is widely observed that families with girls and families with boys are different kinds of families. Most parents agree on that. It is possible that families with two girls, in deciding to have a third child, are not seeking a boy but find children a pleasure and, since two are not too many, they look forward to a third; however, a family with two boys may face a different noise level, or be slightly less satisfied with family life, or, equally satisfied, be more impressed that two is a large number. Or maybe boys and girls have a different affect on relations between the spouses or anything else (like the divorce rate) that has a statistical influence on the birth of a third child. In other words, we couldn't be sure that we were observing preferences for either boys or girls if we did find some of these differences in the census figures.

Furthermore, there are at least two ways that preferences might change if the choice became an actuality. There are many cultures in which boy babies are a sign of virility or of God's favor; there is a slightly coercive tradition that fathers want boys, and the congratulations sound more self-assured when the father has announced a boy. Even grandparents have been known to offer condolences when a third child is a third girl. All of that may evaporate once it's known that the sex of the baby indicates nothing more than whether the mother took a blue pill or a pink pill. The father who insists he really is glad that his second child is a girl like the first won't be thought merely keeping his chin up if it's clear that, had he wanted a boy, he could have had one.

And a new set of social and demographic influences will come to bear on the choice if parents have to observe and anticipate sex ratios that depart from the approximate 50–50 in which boys and girls have traditionally been born. If the sex ratio within the ethnic groups or region or social class with which parents identify their children for school, marriage, and career, departs substantially from the historical ratios, and especially if there are government programs to tilt the incentives, people will have to think about the relative merits of being in the majority or minority sex. How they would make those calculations is at present just more speculation, but it is a fair guess that they would make them. If the little boy reports that two-thirds of his kindergarten class are little boys and only one-third girls, his parents will reflect on those figures before deciding whether their next should be a girl or a boy.

Will people be glad to have this choice available? Or will it just add one more decision to make, one more source of conflict, one more opportunity for remorse, when life is already full enough of decisions and married couples have enough to disagree about?

Demographically, the main effects will be the aggregates— the overall sex ratio, or the ratio within particular age groups, ethnic groups, socio-economic groups, and other groups within which social life and marriage occur. But there could be effects on family itself, although it is hard to know how to appraise them. For example, if the main direction of choice were toward balanced families—a boy and a girl in two-child families—fewer boys would have brothers and fewer girls would have sisters, more boys would have sisters and more girls would have brothers. With today's technology, half the boys in two-child families have brothers; with a technology that leads to mixed families, none of them would.

For the overall ratio, we can do a little arithmetic to get an idea of the differences that various choices could make. A preference that appears to show up in interviews and questionnaires in America and Western Europe is a desire for at least one boy. This sounds like a modest male preference, but may not indicate a preference at all if people also wish to have at least one girl. There has also been occasionally observed in the surveys of hypothetical preferences some desire to have a boy first. These two choices could reflect the same preference: if you want at least one boy, a boy first relieves the suspense.

To get a feeling for the arithmetic, consider what would happen if every family elected a boy first. The result depends on whether the choice is to have a boy first and leave it to luck thereafter, or a boy first and balance out with a girl. The arithmetic also depends on how many families end up with a single child, how many with two or three or four. Suppose every family had first a boy and subsequent children at random. The one-child families would be all male, the two-child families would be three-quarters male, the three-child families would be two-thirds male, and so forth. Given the family sizes in this country, the children born in that fashion would be 70 percent male and 30 percent female, a ratio greater than two-to-one. If every family had first a boy and then alternated girls and boys so an even-numbered family would have equal numbers and an odd-numbered family one more boy than the girls, births would be 60 percent boys and 40 percent girls. In this population, no girl would be without a brother; three-fifths of the girls would have no sisters and a third of the boys would have no brothers.

Suppose all families want at least one boy but will take what the lottery gives them until the last child and then, if they do not yet have a boy, choose a boy. Except for families that know in advance that they want only one child—and these are far fewer than the 21 percent in the United States that actually have only one living child—the effect will be small; only families that would have ended up all girls will be affected, and they will have a single boy in place of a girl—and even that will not happen in families that stop having children before they complete their plan.

What are the consequences of an imbalance in the sex ratio? Of all our institutions, monogamous marriage is the one most directly concerned. But in that regard there are already imbalances. First, there are geographical differences ranging from an excess of women in the Washington area to a large excess of men in some Western states and especially Hawaii and Alaska. Second, young women of an age to marry have recently outnumbered young men of an age to marry in this country because of the tendency for husbands to be older than wives at first marriage; with new births increasing at 3 percent per year, as they did for the quarter century that ended in 1956, a three-year age difference means that the women are drawn from a more recent population that is almost 10 percent larger. Third, women live longer than men in this country, and there is a large excess of unmarried women over unmarried men. The ratio is nearly 4 to 1 in the age group beginning at 45. The difference in life expectancy for men and women in their early twenties is six or seven years; and the young woman who marries a man three years older can expect on average to outlive him by a full decade. Evidently the near equality of male and female births coexists with sizable imbalances for important age groups.

What does the government do, as a matter of policy, if boys and girls are born in very unequal numbers, or even if the ratio fluctuates in cycles, evening out in the long run but leaving large alternating imbalances in successive age groups? At the level of "technical policy," the problem is probably no harder than coping with inflation or unemployment, energy, changes in the birth rate, or changes in the ratio of elderly retired to the working population. The government could attempt to "stabilize" the birth ratio by a variety of fiscal measures, like differential income tax deductions, differential eligibility of men and women for military service, arrangements for differential college tuition, and a variety of favoritisms and affirmative actions discriminating by sex. It wouldn't be easy to devise successful policies, but it wouldn't be analytically different from so many things that the government presently tries to stabilize.

But the social and even constitutional implications are awesome. Imagine the government's having to have a policy on a "target" sex ratio for births. Imagine that Presidential candidates had to debate whether it's better for men to exceed women by 5 percent or 10 percent or not at all, or for women to exceed men. Besides the need to incorporate a multitude of sexually discriminatory rewards and penalties throughout the government's expenditure and revenue and regulatory programs, there would have to be a policy on the "correct" numbers of men and women to have.

There are already people who argue that federal programs to help the poor with family planning have racial implications, even racial motives. Imagine having explicit demographic targets: a President proposing measures that would hold inflation to 4 percent, unemployment to 5 percent, and excess little boys to 6 percent.

So it isn't only parents who might like to be spared some of the choices that would have to be made if this particular technology became available. There are some things—the weather may be one, and the sex of a child at birth another—that it is a great relief to be unable to control. The lottery dispenses arbitrary justice indiscriminately, but it may beat having to discriminate.

Other Characteristics for Selection

What are some other characteristics you might want to consider?

Body size?
Longevity?
Ethnic identity?
Left- or right-handedness?
Eyesight?
Athletic ability?
IQ?
Baldheadedness?

The technology of choice may differ for these different characteristics. Some characteristics relate to continuous variables, like longevity or body size, others to discrete characteris-

tics like left-handedness or perhaps baldness. Some of the discrete choices, like certain "pathologies," may involve screening
for an identifiable unique characteristic; other choices will
involve choosing an extreme or average value along a scale.
Some choices may be uniquely identified with a particular
chromosome; others may tend to "cluster" in a single chromosome but not exclusively; and the determinants of some may
be distributed among several chromosomes. Physiognomy, for
example, may tend to "cluster" more than, say, longevity.
Finally, two or more important characteristics may be determined by the same chromosomes, making it hard to choose
these characteristics independently.

Some Demographic Consequences of Choice

If most parents for several generations tried to have children just a little larger than most other people, we'd eventually
get rather big—"we" the human race, not we the twentieth-
century parents. And what the world is going to need in the future is smaller people, not larger ones. Even if you decide you
are not much interested in body size but merely want your child
not below the lower decile, and if everybody makes *that*
choice, there will be a significant effect on average body size.
The expectation that other parents are going to be selecting
somewhat taller children could make parents who would otherwise be willing to take potluck hedge a little in anticipation,
and avoid children who would have been moderately short in
the parents' generation but might be noticeably below average
in their own generation. The result could be analogous to more
familiar kinds of inflation.

Some Cultural Consequences of Selection

If most of you don't much care whether your child is right-
or left-handed but, given a choice, slightly prefer the child not
be left-handed in case it becomes unfashionable, and, if it is

easy to choose right-handedness, you may participate in converting left-handedness from a common, innocuous characteristic—even a source of pride—to one so rare that, in order not to inflict that kind of rarity on a child, people would avoid it. A normal characteristic could become a stigma through a myriad of uncoordinated individual choices.

Prediction as Guesswork

This is necessarily a conjectural topic. Whatever our uncertainty about development of the technology and about the chromosomal choices that the technology may discover, there is at least as much uncertainty—not a lack of ingredients for conjecture but a profusion of casual data good for nothing but conjecture—about the choices that people might elect to make, about the expectations people would have about other people's choices and any inducements that would arise from those expectations, about the attitudes and professional advice that would be brought to bear on personal decisions or about the policies that governmental and religious bodies might promote, and about the ways that decisions may be made—decisions that would usually involve a minimum of two persons, the parents, and often more.

It is even difficult to guess which choices might seem deadly serious and which frivolous when the time came. I imagine that the bottom item on my list, baldheadedness, will appear frivolous. Perusal of advertisements suggests that it is an almost, but not quite, innocuous "pathology." Exploratory speculation about social processes, like choosing characteristics of one's children, sometimes gains a little freedom by focusing on choices that are not too serious. Baldheadedness may be an example of a culturally determined "aesthetic" choice, one that can serve as a proxy for "looks" or "beauty" and that might be highly responsive to the frequency rate within the population, and one that is correlated with sex. It may be illustrative of how discrimination and stigmata are generated in a culture.

The Contrast with Traditional Eugenics

Baldheadedness is furthermore illustrative of a striking difference between the older-fashioned eugenics and the futuris-
tic possibility of chromosomal selection. The difference is this.
Eugenics, like animal husbandry, selects *parents*; what we are
now discussing is the selection of particular chromosomes from
the parents. Traditional eugenics—by which I mean almost any
program that might have been proposed for "choosing our children's genes" a generation ago—involved a yes-no decision
whether or not a person should be a parent. (This was not true
in animal husbandry because the offspring could be selectively
destroyed, sterilized, or prevented from further breeding.) It
therefore involved interference in one of the most personal
rights that a person could claim. Chromosomal selection of the
kind discussed now is more benign. It can be opportunistic,
and it can be at the choice of the parents. A "dominant" trait
of one parent can be screened out with about a fifty-fifty
chance of success by the second try. And if sperm can be
screened, a dominant trait can be selected out of an abundant
population of sperm at no cost to the father, except to the
extent that the trait selected out may involve a chromosome
that one would have preferred on other grounds, such as sex of
the child. Recessive traits located in chromosomes that carry a
"signature" that can be identified with particular ancestors
could similarly be avoided. With respect to serious pathologies, the liberation from a choice between grave risk and child-
lessness would be enormous—and in some cases already is. The
principle applies to the frivolous as well.

Probably the most important constraint is that some characteristics may be determined by the chromosome that determines the sex of the child; this is a good example of "cluster-
ing" within the chromosome. It is also a good example of the
special, if not unique, significance of the choice of sex. If a
couple wants a boy, or a girl, it is restricted to the characteristics determined by the chromosome that determines sex.

Some Motivational and Demographic Configurations

The motives for choosing particular traits or measures can be quite diverse. Some traits may be objects of avoidance because they are painful or awkward or fearsome irrespective of their frequency in the population or their cultural status; these would be the unconditional pathologies.

Then there may be traits that are dangerous or disagreeable primarily because they are rare or represent extreme values on a distribution. Some of these, but not all of them, are disagreeable because they are socially stigmatized. (A few traits may be valuable precisely because they are rare, may even have economic value because of scarcity.) An important distinction is between the traits one would choose, or the value along some scale that one would choose, independently of the frequencies and averages of the relevant surrounding population, and the choices that are substantially conditioned by one's human environment. Preferred body size must be substantially conditioned: one wants to see over the top of the grass but, if the whole population could be scaled accordingly, it takes a while to decide whether one would rather be three feet tall or six.

Some but not all of this conditioning by the human surroundings is competitive: one wants to be about normal size to find clothes and chairs and stair risers that one can accommodate comfortably, but also may prefer to be a little larger or a little stronger or a little taller than others because of some advantage. In the competitive cases one confers a disadvantage on others by successfully achieving the advantage of being larger than they; in contrast, musical talent may be something that people enjoy in the surrounding population, and having a musically talented child may benefit its friends and put them to no disadvantage.

But the conditioned choices can be to conform or to disperse or to identify, not merely to "fit" or to "excel." One might, for example, want a child to be average in complexion, different in hair color, taller than average, like or unlike one's ethnic group, long-lived but not precocious in development.

These different kinds of preferences could produce quite different dynamic trends. Longevity, if it does not come at the expense of some other desirable characteristic, is likely to be highly valued, especially if it amounts to the avoidance of short-livedness. And the non-natural selection exercised by parents in behalf of their children could increase the mean life span by working on some part or all of the frequency distribution. The prospect of longer-lived spouses and companions might make a long life appear even more worthwhile.

It is harder to guess what would happen to facial and other visible ethnic characteristics. Individual choices might bring about either ethnic blending or ethnic differentiation.

IQ might be treated as a competitive trait; valuable as it may be for its own sake, it may be construed particularly valuable in a competitive society, whether the competition is based on IQ measurements themselves, on the school success to which IQ may contribute, or on competitive success in one's career. If it were widely believed that the genetic mixtures within most parents made it possible by chromosomal selection to raise the expected IQ of a child by many points above what it would have been by chance selection of the chromosomes; and if it became widely believed in certain social classes that nearly everybody was taking advantage of this opportunity; parents might feel coerced into practicing selection not out of any dissatisfaction with the prospective intelligence of their children, but to keep up with the new generation.

Choosing for Whom?

An interesting difference between longevity and IQ is that IQ may focus attention on the *child* that one's baby will become and longevity on the *adult* it will be eventually. If longevity is determined by chromosomes unrelated to IQ, the hardness of choice will depend on whether one is picking an optimal combination of IQ and longevity from among millions of sperm or, instead, considering abortion of a fetus on the basis of its prospective IQ and longevity. The parents, who are about to have a baby, are probably thinking more about the child it will be than about the old man or woman it will eventually become.

At the same time, these parents are not themselves children. The father may not expect to have a baldheaded schoolboy, but if he's old enough to do a little estate planning at the prospect of an enlarged family he may be thinking of *his* life and what he would wish for himself if he could wish for the things he is about to choose for his child.

Some Consequences of Having a Choice

There are at least two respects in which an ability to choose chromosomes might be unwelcome. One is that some of the things that we might be most motivated to choose have the quality that if we all choose what we individually prefer we are all a little worse off. The illustration I have used is body size. It may be an advantage to be a little larger than others; it is no collective advantage to have the average height and body size move up.

Some minor nuisances could become stigmata if they became less common, without disappearing altogether, through a massive "unpopularity contest." A few examples are no proof that the collective social and demographic consequences would outweigh the gains, but the examples remind us that there is nothing about externally conditioned, voluntary choices that guarantees they lead to any collective benefit.

The other difficulty is within the family itself. An example is the choice of the sex of the baby. This is one more thing for the prospective parents to be in disagreement about, with each other and with the grandparents. (If the technique of choice is at all unsure, they run the risk of getting a girl or a boy after together committing themselves to a preference for a boy or a girl.) The family that already has a boy and a girl and plans on one more may be almost in the position of delivering a "verdict," in the presence of two children, after trying one of each.

The skinny boy whose mother insists on violin lessons may wonder whether "he" might not have been big like the other boys if his mother hadn't traded size for musical talent before he was old enough to be asked what he preferred. And he may not be satisfied with the answer that "he" comes in only one size: the alternative was some other little boy or girl from among those sixty trillion.

7

HOCKEY HELMETS, DAYLIGHT SAVING, AND OTHER BINARY CHOICES

S HORTLY after Teddy Green of the Bruins took a hockey stick in his brain, *Newsweek* (October 6, 1969), commented:

Players will not adopt helmets by individual choice for several reasons. Chicago star Bobby Hull cites the simplest factor: "Vanity." But many players honestly believe that helmets will cut their efficiency and put them at a disadvantage, and others fear the ridicule of opponents. The use of helmets will spread only through fear caused by injuries like Green's—or through a rule making them mandatory. . . . One player summed up the feelings of many: "It's foolish not to wear a helmet. But I don't—because the other guys don't. I know that's silly, but most of the players feel the same way. If the league made us do it, though, we'd all wear them and nobody would mind."

The *Newsweek* story went on to quote Don Awrey. "When I saw the way Teddy looked, it was an awful feeling. . . . I'm going to start wearing a helmet now, and I don't care what anybody says." But viewers of Channel 38 (Boston) know that Awrey did not.

This chapter is about binary choices with externalities. These are either-or situations. An "externality" occurs if you care about my choice or my choice affects yours. You may not care but need to know: whether to pass on left or right when we meet. Or you may not need to know but care: you will drive whether or not I drive, but prefer that I keep off the road.[13]

Paying or not paying your share is an example, or wearing

[13] "Externality" is not the term I would coin for this book but it is fixed in economics and you will have to be familiar with it. It refers to the effects of a firm's actions, or an agency's or a person's, that are beyond and outside—"external to"—the firm's accounting or the agency's purview or the person's interests and concerns, but within the accounting, the purview, or the interest of somebody else.

a helmet in a hockey game. So is keeping your dog leashed, voting yes on ERA, staying in the neighborhood or moving out, joining a boycott, signing a petition, getting vaccinated, carrying a gun, or liability insurance, or a tow cable; driving with headlights up or down, riding a bicycle to work, shoveling the sidewalks in front of your house, or going on daylight saving. The question is not how *much* anyone does but how *many* make the one choice or the other.

Joining a self-restraining coalition, or staying out and doing what's done naturally, is a binary choice. If we contemplate all the restraints that a coalition might impose, the problem is multifarious; but if the coalition is there, and its rules have been adopted, the choice to join or not to join is binary. Ratifying a nuclear treaty or confirming a Supreme Court justice is multifarious until the treaty is drafted or the justice nominated; there then remains, usually, a binary choice.[14]

In some cases the arrangement matters. If everybody needs 100 watts to read by and a neighbor's bulb is equivalent to half one's own, and everybody has a 60-watt bulb, everybody can read as long as he and both his neighbors have their lights on. Arranged in a circle, everybody will keep his light on if everybody else does (and nobody will if his neighbors do not); arranged in a line, the people at the ends cannot read anyway and turn their lights off, and the whole thing unravels. Here we'll consider only situations in which people are identically situated. Everybody's outcome, whichever way he makes his choice, depends only on the *number* of people who choose one way or the other.

---

[14] An intriguing account of complex interdependencies with $n =$ 101 and an almost-binary choice—absence and abstention being possible alternatives—with varying degrees of reversibility of choice, incomplete and sometimes manipulated information, small networks of special influence, and non-uniform preferences among the participants, is Richard Harris' story of the Senate's action on Judge Carswell, "Annals of Politics," *The New Yorker*, December 5 and 12, 1970, and *Decision*, Ballantine Books, Inc., 1971.

Knowledge and Observation

If people need to know how others are choosing, to make their own choices, it will matter whether or not they can find out what everybody is doing. I can tell how many people have snow tires if I look around; it is harder to know how many cars that pass me in an emergency have tow chains. I have no way of knowing who is vaccinated, unless I ask people to roll up their sleeves; but my doctor can find the statistics and tell me. I have a good idea how many people regularly wear ties and jackets to the faculty dining club hall; but going to a party it is hard to find out, until after I have made my choice and go, how many people are going black-tie, or in sneakers.

Continuous or repeated binary-choice activities, when they are easily visible and there are no costs in switching, may allow easy, continuous adjustment to what others are doing. Once-for-all choices are often taken in the dark. Some choices, like resigning in protest, are necessarily visible; some, like loaded guns and vaccination scars, can be revealed or concealed; some, like fouling or not fouling a public pond, may be not only invisible but unrevealable. For discipline and enforcement it will usually matter whether individual choices or only the aggregates or percentages can be monitored. Unless I say otherwise, I shall usually have in mind that people can see and adapt to the choices of others; but we should keep in mind that this is a special case, and often an especially easy one to deal with.

What people actually "see and adapt to" is sometimes not the number of choices one way or the other but the consequences. While the senator who considers voting against the President's nominee for the Supreme Court probably cares directly about the number of negative votes, the owner of the double-parked automobile is more interested in the safety in numbers than in the numbers themselves. Parents who decline vaccination for their children should be interested in how much safety the vaccination of others provides, not in the numbers themselves, although they may have a more reliable estimate of numbers than of risk. The distinction between numbers per se and their consequences—which it is that one cares about, and also which it is that one can observe—is a distinction that ought, in a particular case, to be explicit; but I shall usually speak as though it is the choices themselves that a person can see and that he cares about.

What we have, then, is a population of n individuals, each with a choice between L and R ("Left" and "Right") corresponding in our diagrammatic analysis to the two directions on a horizontal scale or, in an actual choice, to the two sides of a road, or two political parties. For any individual the payoff to a choice of L or R depends on how many others choose Left or Right.

Prisoner's Dilemma

A good place to begin is the situation known—in its two-person version—as "prisoner's dilemma." It involves a binary choice for each of two people and can be described as follows:

1. Each has an *unconditional preference:* the same choice is preferred, irrespective of which choice the other person makes.
2. Each has an *unconditional preference* with respect to the *other's choice:* this preference for the other person's action is unaffected by the choice one makes for oneself.
3. These two preferences go in *opposite* directions: the choice that each prefers to make is not the choice he prefers the other to make.
4. The strengths of these preferences are such that both are better off making their unpreferred choices than if both make their preferred choices.

An illustrative matrix is in Figure 13. One person, R for "Row," makes a choice that can be represented as a choice of

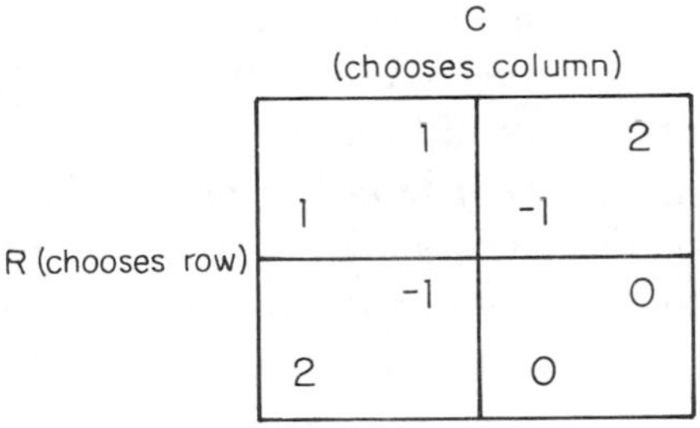

C
(chooses column)

	1	2
1		-1
	-1	0
2		0

R (chooses row)

NOTE: Lower-left number in each cell denotes the payoff to R (choosing row), upper-right number the payoff to C (choosing column)

Figure 13

upper or lower row; C ("Column") chooses left- or right-hand column. The lower-left number in a cell of the matrix denotes the payoff value to R, the upper-right number the payoff to C. R prefers the lower row irrespective of C's choice, and C the right-hand column whatever R chooses. That way both get zero. If both make "unpreferred" choices, they get the upper-left cell for 1 apiece; each could gain a point there, at a cost of two points to the other, by switching to the preferred row or column.

That situation is a fairly simple one to define. But when we turn to the multi-person version, the definition is ambiguous. "Other" is "all others" when there are only two; with more than two there are in-between possibilities. We have to elaborate the definition in a way that catches the spirit of prisoner's dilemma, and see whether we then have something distinctive enough to be assigned a proper name.

Extending the Definition

There are two main definitional questions. (1) Is an individual always better off, the more there are among the others who choose their unpreferred alternative? (2) Does the individual's own preference remain constant no matter how many among the others choose one way or the other? Tentatively answering yes, for purposes of definition, to these two questions, and assuming that *only numbers matter* (not people's identities), and that all payoff rankings are the same for all players, a *uniform multi-person prisoner's dilemma*—henceforth MPD for short—can be defined as a situation in which:

1. There are n people, each with the same binary choice and the same payoffs.
2. Each has a preferred choice whatever the others do; and the same choice is preferred by everybody.
3. Whichever choice a person makes, he or she is better off, the more there are among the others who choose their unpreferred alternative.
4. There is some number, k, greater than 1, such that if individuals numbering k or more choose their unpreferred alternative and the rest do not, those who do are better off than if they had all chosen their preferred alternatives, but if they number less than k this is not true.

Taking the four numbered statements as a plausible extension of the prisoner's-dilemma idea, and as what I shall mean by MPD, we have at first glance an important parameter k. It represents the minimum size of any coalition that can gain by abstaining from the preferred choice. It is the smallest disciplined group that, though resentful of the free riders, can be profitable for those who join (though more profitable for those who stay out).

On a horizontal axis measured from 0 to n, two payoff curves are drawn. (I switch, for convenience, to a population of $n + 1$, so that "n" is the number of "others" there are for any one person.) One curve corresponds to the preferred choice; its left end is arbitrarily taken as zero point, and it rises to the right, perhaps leveling off but not declining. Below it we draw the curve for the unpreferred choice. It begins below 0, rises and crosses the axis at some point denoted by k. We use L ("Left") to stand for the preferred alternative and R ("Right") for the unpreferred. The number choosing Right is

denoted by the distance of any point rightward from the left
end. At a horizontal value of $n/3$, one third of the way from
left to right, the two curves show the value to a person of
choosing L or R when one-third of the others choose R and
two-thirds choose L.

Figure 14 shows several curves that meet the definition.
The only constraints on these curves are that the four extrem-
ities of the two curves be in the vertical order shown and that
the curves rise to the right and not cross. Matching the pic-
tures in Figure 14 with actual situations is good exercise but I
leave it to you. In A the disadvantage of a Right choice is constant; in B the cost of a Right choice grows with the number
making that choice, L benefiting more than R from the
externality.

The "values" accruing to Right and Left choices for different individuals may or may not be susceptible to some
common measure. Reactions to smells, noises, and other irri-
tants cannot be summed over the population. Even if there is a
common measure—frequency of illness, time lost in waiting in
line, busy signals on the telephone—an indiscriminate summation may produce a total of little interest. But there are cases
in which some measurable total is of interest. Even without
supposing that my time is as valuable as yours, it can make
sense to inquire about the total amount of lost time between
us. And often a simple total can be taken to represent an
appropriately weighted sum, if there is no expected correlation
between the weights one would attach to different individuals
and their likely choices of Left and Right. The dotted lines in
Figure 14 show the total values (or average values) corresponding to the numbers choosing Right and Left. At the left
end of the scale, everybody is choosing Left, and the total (or
average) coincides with the Left curve. On the right-hand
side, it coincides with the Right curve. Midway between left
and right sides it is midway vertically between the curves, and
at the one-third and two-thirds marks it is located at one-third
of the vertical distance, or two-thirds of the vertical distance,
from curve L to curve R.

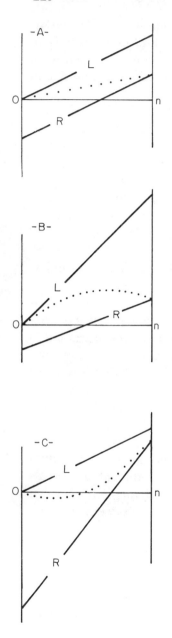

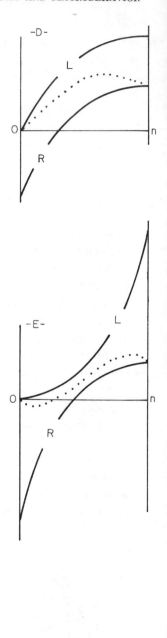

Figure 14

The Significant Parameters

In the description of MPD a crucial parameter is k, the minimum size of a viable coalition. "Viable" means that on an either-or basis, assuming that nobody else cooperates, some group of cooperators can benefit from choosing the Right strategy if their number is up to k. This is the minimum-sized coalition that makes sense all by itself. Evidently it takes more than one parameter to describe one of these MPD situations: Figure 14 suggests how much they can differ even if k is held constant. But staying with k for the moment, we might ask whether we shouldn't focus on k/n, or, for that matter, $n-k$.

If n is fixed, they come to the same thing. But n can vary from situation to situation, so the question whether k, k/n, or $n-k$ is the controlling parameter is not a matter of definition. It depends on what the situation is.

If k is the number of whaling vessels that abide by an international ration on the capture of whales, the crucial thing will probably not be k but $n-k$. If enough people whale indiscriminately, there is no number of restrained whalers who will be better off by restraining themselves. If there is an infinitely elastic supply of cars for the turnpike, no matter how many among us restrict our driving we will not reduce congestion. And so forth.

On the other hand, if the whalers want a lighthouse and the problem is to cover its cost, they need only a coalition big enough to spread the cost thin enough to make the lighthouse beneficial to those who pay their shares. If the value of the lighthouse to each boat is independent of how many benefit, whalers numbering k or more can break even or better by sharing the costs, no matter how many enjoy the light free of charge.

And if it is proportions that matter—the fraction of vessels carrying some emergency equipment—k will vary proportionately with n. So we have a second characteristic of the uniform MPD: the relation between k and n.

A third is what happens to the difference in value between Left and Right. Does the incentive to choose Left—to stay out of the coalition—increase or decrease with the size of the coalition? The more the rest of you restrict your whaling, the more whales I catch by staying out of the self-restraining coalition if entry into the whaling industry is limited and I am already in the business. Alternatively, if joining a coalition means only paying my share of the lighthouse, it becomes cheaper as more join.

We can measure this by the change in the vertical distance between our two curves with the number who choose Right. In Figure 14 some of the curves open toward the right, showing an increasing difference, and some taper with a diminishing difference.

There is a fourth important parameter if we treat these payoff values as additive numbers. This is the number choosing Right that *maximizes the total value* (denoted, in Figure 14, by the highest point on the dotted curve). If the rationing scheme is too strict, whalers may collectively get more whales or make more profit if some choose Left, that is, some stay out. The optimum number to be vaccinated against smallpox will usually be less than the entire population, because the risk of infection is proportionate to the number vaccinated while the epidemiological benefits taper off before 100 percent.

In some cases, collective maximization ought to occur only when all choose Right if the terms of the coalition have been properly set. It would be silly to have a limit of one deer per season if the rangers then had to go out and hunt down the excess deer. It makes sense to set the limit so that deer hunters are best off when all abide, rather than relying on some free riders to cull the herd. But sometimes the thing cannot be arranged; it may be hard to devise a scheme that allows everybody one and one-third deer per season.

A conflict of interest intervenes then. Consider vaccination: if the optimal number is 90 percent of the population and nobody can be nine-tenths vaccinated, there has to be a system to determine who gets vaccinated. (Actually, people can be "fractionally" vaccinated, through longer intervals between revaccinations with some lapse of immunity.) With turnpikes and deer hunters one can search for a quantitative readjustment that makes optimum benefits coincide with universal membership, even if people have to be allowed four deer every three years to take care of the fractions.

There has not been a case of smallpox in the United States since 1949, and it is now believed to have disappeared in the rest of the world. Complications from the vaccine cause an occasional death and mild allergic reactions in about one vaccination out of a thousand. The Public Health Service no longer recommends routine vaccination of youngsters. Because immunity wanes, many adults who were once vaccinated may be unprotected now.

Suppose the Public Health Service announced that, considering together the disease and its contagion and the hazards of vaccination, optimally the United States population should be two-thirds vaccinated. What do you elect for your children? (Suppose it simultaneously mentions that if, as is *nationally* optimal, two-thirds of the population is vaccinated, it is *individually* better to be unvaccinated!)

There can be more conflict if the collective maximum occurs to the left of k. Unless a distributive problem can be solved, achievement of a collective maximum then entails net losses, not merely lesser gains, for those who choose Right. If choosing right is voluntary, all-or-none, and non-compensable, any viable coalition has to be inefficiently large.

It is worth noticing that a coalition—even an involuntary coalition—can change payoffs by its mere existence. In a recent article on high school proms the author described the reaction, when she tried to make tuxedos optional, of "the boys who wouldn't, on their own, go out and rent a tux, but who like the idea of being forced to wear one. . . . For many this would be the only time they'd have an excuse to dress up." Remember Bobby Hull's diagnosis of the aversion to helmets: vanity. A voluntary helmet may be seen as cowardly, but nobody thinks a baseball player timid when he dons the batting helmet that the league won't let him play without. Motorcycle helmets are not only worn regularly, but probably worn more gladly, in states that require them. I shall continue to assume in this chapter that payoffs depend only on the choices and not on the way the choices are brought about, but the reader is alerted to alternative possibilities.

I have used "coalition" to mean those who are induced to choose Right. They may do it through enforceable contract, or someone's coercing them, or in the belief that if they do others will but not if they don't, or by a golden rule.

But "coalition" often has an institutional definition. It is a subset of the population that has enough structure to arrive at a collective decision for its members, or for some among them, or for all of them with some probability, in this particular binary choice. They can be members of a union or a trade association or a faculty or a gun club or a veterans' organization, who elect to act as a unit in a political campaign, in abiding by some rule, in making a contribution, or in joining some larger confederation. And this could take either of two forms, disciplining *individual* choices of the members or making a *collective* choice on behalf of them.

↓
→ to here in Barry + Hardin

Some Different Configurations

Until now we have looked only at MPD. We have to look at cases in which the curves either cross, with equilibria at their intersection or at their end points, or slope in opposite directions. We have to look at situations in which people want to do what everybody else does, and in which people want to avoid what everybody else does.

But first let's remind outselves why the prisoner's dilemma gets as much attention as it does. Its fascination is that it generates an *inefficient equilibrium*: There is one way that everybody can act so that everybody is doing what is in his own best interest given what everybody else is doing, yet *all* could be better off if they *all* made opposite choices. This calls for some effort at social organization, some way to collectivize the choice or to strike an enforceable bargain or otherwise to re-structure incentives so that people will do the opposite of what they naturally would have done.

When the number of people is large, though, the prisoner's dilemma is not special in that respect. We can draw a number of R-choice and L-choice curves that generate inefficient equilibria and that do not have the shapes or slopes or end-point configurations of MPD.

So we should probably identify as the generic problem, not the inefficient equilibrium of prisoner's dilemma, but all the situations in which equilibria achieved by unconcerted or undisciplined action are inefficient—the situations in which everybody could be better off, or some collective total could be made larger, by concerted or disciplined or organized or regulated or centralized decisions.

And among those situations we shall find a major division between (1) the superior choice that is self-enforcing once arrived at—the situation in which people prefer one of two quite different equilibria but can be trapped at the less attractive of the two—and (2) the superior choice that requires coercion, enforceable contract, centralization of choice, or some way to make everybody's choice conditional on everybody else's. The MPD is then a special, but not very special, sub-class of those that require enforcement of a non-equilibrium choice.

It should be kept in mind that, for people in an MPD or like situation, organizing a disciplined choice is *their* problem, not necessarily ours. "They" can be racketeers enforcing a code of silence, bigots organizing a boycott, conspirators organizing a monopoly, or political opponents forming a caucus against us.

Intersecting Curves

To fit MPD into this larger classification, take a straightline version of MPD—*B* in Figure 14, for example—and shift the Right curve up as in Figure 15. It crosses what used to be the "upper" curve, and Left is no longer unconditionally preferred. At the left, with only a few choosing Right, Right is preferred. If we suppose any kind of orderly adjustment, we have a *stable equilibrium* at the intersection.[15] If more than that number choose Right, Left will be the better choice and people will switch from Right to Left until the two are equivalent in value. If fewer choose Right, Right will be the more attractive choice and people will switch from Left to Right until the advantage disappears.

This equilibrium cannot be at a collective maximum. Everybody gains if some choosing Left will choose Right. Those already choosing Right travel upward on *their* curve; and all

---

[15] More exactly the equilibrium is located as follows. Let X be the number choosing Right. (X is a whole number.) With straight lines for the L and R curves, $L = aX + b$ and $R = cX + d$; they intersect where $L = R$, or $X = (d - b)/(a - c)$. (Because the L curve is steeper and begins below the R curve on the left side, both numerator and denominator are positive.) Equilibrium occurs where there is no gain in switching from a choice of L to a choice of R or from R to L. Switching from L to R raises the number choosing R by one, so the first condition is that $aX + b \geqq c(X + 1) + d$; this transposes to $X \geqq (d - b + c)/(a - c)$, which is a distance of $c/(a - c)$ to the right of the intersection at $(d - b)/(a - c)$. Switching from R to L reduces by one the number choosing Right, so the second condition is that $a(X - 1) + B \leqq cX + d$; this transposes to $X \leqq (d - b + a)/(a - c)$, which is a distance of $a/(a - c)$ to the right of the intersection. The equilibrium value of X thus falls in a range that is one unit wide—the difference between the upper and lower limits is $(a - c)/(a - c)$—and that begins $c/(a - c)$ to the right of the intersection. There is a unique integer-value of X in the one-unit range (unless the end points coincide with two adjacent integers, in which case there are two indifferent equilibrium values, a person able to switch from one to the other and back without gaining or losing). To illustrate, if the L curve is twice as steep as the R curve the equilibrium is somewhere from one to two units to the right of the intersection. If the population is large the difference between the equilibrium and the intersection is too small to distinguish on the printed diagram.

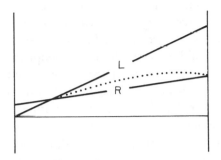

Figure 15

who switch from Left to Right arrive at a higher point on the
Right curve than where they were at "equilibrium." (The
collective maximum can occur short of the right extremity.)

Does this differ much from MPD? Both offer an equilibrium that is inferior for everybody to *any* greater number
choosing Right.

What distinguishes MPD is simply that, at the MPD equilibrium, *nobody* is choosing Right; in the intersecting case,
with both curves rising to the right; *somebody* is. But the difference is not much. In either case the equilibrium is inefficient: all are better off choosing Right than congregating at
the equilibrium. And in either case the collective maximum
can involve fewer than the whole population choosing Right.

(There is no need for everybody to have a tow cable in his
car trunk. It takes two cars to need a cable, and two cables are
no better than one. The "carry" *R* curve should be nearly horizontal; the "don't carry" *L* curve could begin substantially
beneath it, curve over and cross it, and become parallel toward
the right extremity, at a vertical distance equal to the cost of
the cable. The intersection would be an equilibrium if people
could respond to an observed frequency of cables in the car
population. Because the "carry" curve is horizontal, the equilibrium is just as good as if everybody bought and carried a

cable, and no better; the collectively superior position would entail a greater frequency of cables, but short of 100 percent. Because of the curvature, a shortfall of cables below the equilibrium value could be severe for the L people.)

In Figure 15 the *Left* choice is preferred at the *right* (where most people are choosing Right) and the *Right* choice at the *left* (where most people are choosing Left). Keeping both curves sloping up to the right and intersecting, we could have the two curves interchanged: a Right choice preferred at the right and a Left choice at the left. This is the case in Figure 4. There we have two equilibria, an all-Right choice and an all-Left. The right one, enjoying the externality, is the better. But, if everybody chooses left, nobody is motivated to choose otherwise unless enough others do to get over the hump and beyond the intersection.

In Figure 16, L can stand for carrying a visible weapon, R for going unarmed. I may prefer to be armed if everybody else is but not if the rest are not. (These may be nuclear weapons, and the "individuals" nations?) The *visibility* of weapons can have two effects. If L and R are as in Figure 4, you don't know where you are on your curve—whichever curve it is—if personal weapons are concealed or if nuclear weapons are clandestine. More likely, visibility will change the payoffs—the

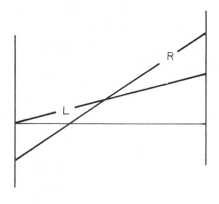

Figure 16

risks or benefits of being armed often depend on whether one is visibly armed. (Reliable weapon checks might help, even if weapons themselves could not be prohibited.)

Conditional Externality

Rotate the Right curve clockwise until it slopes downward with an intersection, as in Figure 17. The externality is not uniform: A Right choice benefits those who choose left, a Left choice those who choose right. But we still have an equilibrium. And it is still not at a collective maximum if payoffs are in some commensurable commodity.

There is a difference. If the collective maximum occurs to the right of the intersection, it is necessarily a maximum in which some—those who choose Right—are not as well off as at the equilibrium, unless compensation occurs or people take turns. This poses a special organizational problem.

Figure 17 yields some insight into the role of information. For concreteness suppose that during a highway emergency there are two routes that drivers are not familiar with. If, in their ignorance, they distribute themselves at random between the two routes, with anything like a fifty-fifty division, they

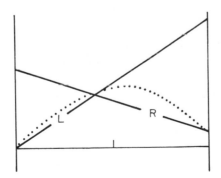

Figure 17

will be to the right of the intersection of the two curves in
Figure 17. Those who chose R would regret it if they knew;
but the outcome is collectively better than an equilibrated
division would have been, and, as a "fair bet," all drivers may
prefer it to a uniform outcome at the intersection. That being
so, the traffic advisor in his helicopter should keep his mouth
shut; he risks diverting just enough traffic to the less congested
route to make both routes equally unattractive. (If we had
drawn the R curve horizontally, the result would be more
striking.) Does the traffic helicopter improve things by telling
all those drivers on the congested routes about the less congested alternates?

Next, let R be staying home and L equal using the car—two
choices after a blizzard. The radio announcer warns everybody
to stay home. Many do, and those who drive are pleasantly
surprised by how empty the roads are; if the others had known,
they would surely have driven. If they had, they would all be
at the lower left extremity of the L curve. An exaggerated
warning can inhibit numbers and may lead to a more nearly
optimal result than a "true" (i.e., a self-confirming) warning,
unless people learn to discount the warning (or subscribe to a
service that keeps them currently informed, so that they all go
to the intersection of the two curves).

Next, keeping the Right curve sloping downward to the
right, but modestly so, displace it downward so that it lies
entirely below the Left curve (Figure 18). There is an equilibrium with all choosing Left. A choice of Right benefits those
who choose Left while a choice of Left benefits those who
choose Right. The situation is unlike MPD because no coalition of Right-choosers can be viable in the absence of compensation. Still, the Left equilibrium can be inefficient. If the
Right curve is not much below the Left curve at the left
extremity, the collective maximum can occur, as it does in
Figure 18, with some choosing Right. We still have the organizational problem of inducing the Right choices that maximize
the collective outcome.

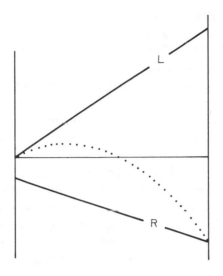

Figure 18

The Commons

This situation has a familiar interpretation. It is "the commons." There are two common grazing grounds, and everybody is free to graze cattle on either one. Alternatively there are two highways, and anybody may drive on either. Anyone who drives on Highway 2 benefits everybody who drives on Highway 1, by reducing congestion there, but adds congestion to Highway 2. Anyone who grazes his cattle on common-pasture 2 adds congestion there, but reduces it on 1. Any problem of congestion with two alternate localities yields the situation represented by two curves that slope in opposite directions.

Dual Equilibria

Turn to the cases of dual equilibria with straight lines.

We have two situations. The curves can have opposite slopes with the Right sloping up to the right and the Left sloping up to the left, so that the externality is conditional and "self-favoring"—a Right choice favoring a Right choice and a Left choice favoring Left. Or both curves can slope up to the right, the Right curve steeper than the Left. (They can both slope up to the left, of course, but that's the same thing with Right and Left interchanged.) Either way, there are two equilibria, one at each extremity. The problem of organization is to achieve the superior equilibrium. If both slope in the same direction, there is no ambiguity about which equilibrium is superior; if they have opposite slopes, either can be the superior one.

In any of these cases with two equilibria, the problem (if there is a problem) is to get a concerted choice, or switch, of enough people to reach the superior equilibrium. There may be no need for coercion, discipline, or centralized choice; it may be enough merely to get people to make the right choice in the first place. If the choice is once-for-all, it is enough to get everybody to expect everybody else to make the right choice, and this expectation may be achieved merely by communication, since nobody has any reason not to make the right choice once there is concerted recognition.

If an inefficient Left choice has become established, no individual will choose Right unless he expects others to do so; this condition will require some organized switch, as in one-way streets or driving to left or right. People can get trapped at an inefficient equilibrium, everyone waiting for the others to switch, nobody willing to be the first unless he has confidence that enough others will switch to make it worthwhile.

Notice now a difference between the curves' both sloping up to the right and their having slopes of opposite sign. In the former, a coalition can occur that is insufficient to induce the remainder to choose Right, yet is viable. Figure 19 illustrates it. If everybody is choosing Left, there is some number, call it k again, that will be better off choosing Right, even though they are too few to make Right the preferred choice for everybody else. The critical number occurs where the Right curve achieves the elevation of the left extremity of the Left curve,

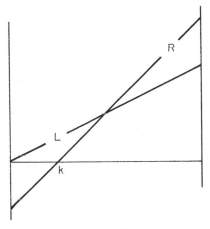

Figure 19

just as in MPD. A Right-choosing coalition is viable if it exceeds this number; if it achieves the larger number corresponding to the intersection, it can induce everybody else to shift. But even if it is too small to accomplish that, the coalition can still benefit. Thus there is an element of MPD even in the situation of two equilibria: there is some coalition that is better off choosing Right, even though the remainder are better off still, and even though any member of the coalition would be better off if he could defect and choose Left. The difference in this case is that there is a still larger coalition that can induce everybody else to switch, because it is big enough to make Right the preferred choice.

MPD as A Truncated Dual Equilibrium

The difference between MPD and the dual equilibria need be no more than a difference in size of population. In Figure 20, with a population of x, there are two equilibria. If k is independent of the population, reduce the population to y and MPD results. Reduce it to z and MPD disappears. The MPD is

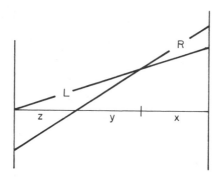

Figure 20

merely a "truncated dual equilibrium," without enough people to carry themselves over the hump. (And the dual equilibrium is merely an "extended MPD," with enough people added to make the coalition self-sustaining.)

Curvatures

There is no end to the shapes we could give our Left-Right curves. But also there is no guarantee that a pair of real choices exists somewhere that corresponds to some pair of curves that we might adopt on heuristic or architectural grounds. Straight lines are somewhat noncommittal and can often serve as proxies for whole families of monotonic curves. But they are somewhat prejudicial in their simplicity: they can intersect only once; and they never reach maxima or minima except at their end points. A few examples with curvature may dispel the presumption that externalities ought to display constant marginal effect.

Uniformity

One interesting class may be U-shaped for both curves, like the three variants in Figure 21.

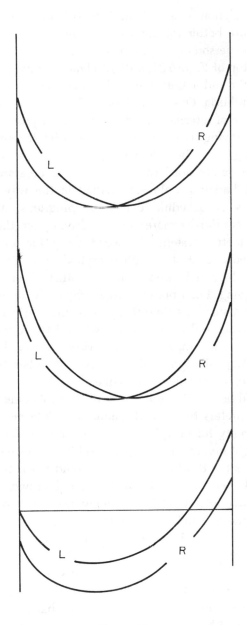

Figure 21

The basic relation is one of "uniformity": uniform choices *for all others* are better for anyone than any mixture, whichever way the one person makes his own choice.

At the top of Figure 21, a Right choice is favored if enough choose Right and a Left choice if enough choose Left. There are two equilibria. One is superior, but either is far better than a wide range of intermediate distributions. A possible instance is daylight saving. Let it be summer and let *R* represent daylight saving. The best is when everybody is on daylight saving. Things are not bad if everybody is on standard time. Things are bad if people are divided in the way they keep office hours or schedule deliveries, programs, and dinner engagements. Furthermore, unlike driving on the right or using the metric system, the worst thing for an individual is not to be out of step with everybody else; it is to have everybody else not in step with each other. Even if I am on daylight saving, I can better navigate my daily life with everybody else on standard time than if half the world joins me in daylight saving and I never know which half. A traveler who crosses time zones may keep his wristwatch on "home time" and get along all right unless he is with other travelers of whom some, but not all, do the same.

The middle case is similar overall. But this time everybody somewhat prefers to be in the minority while mainly preferring uniformity for everybody else. Possibly, to find a parallel with daylight saving, an example could be a choice of Monday or Friday as the third day of the weekend when the four-day work week becomes common. To avoid crowds, one may prefer to have Friday off if everybody else drives out of town or goes to the golf links on Monday. (Or, if it is storekeepers, everybody prefers to be open for business the day his competitors are closed.) At the same time, in getting up a golf game or going to the beach with friends, or just knowing what stores are open and who is keeping office hours, there is advantage in the rest of the world's uniformity; and, on balance, it is better to be in line with everybody else if one cannot enjoy exclusivity. In any event, if equilibrium is reached it is an unsatisfactory one. The temptation to be different stirs things up to everybody's disadvantage.

The case at the bottom shows a single equilibrium, comparatively satisfactory but not completely so. (It could have been drawn with the Left extremity higher than the Right and an efficient outcome. To illustrate a problem, I have drawn it contrary.) Left is the decimal system, Right the duodecimal. Either works fine, but if half of us are on one and half on the other, the result is confusion. Furthermore, it is just hard enough to convert to a duodecimal system that, though on behalf of posterity I wish everybody else would change, in my lifetime I would rather stick to my own system, even if it means I am out of step. As in MPD, I may be willing to adopt the duodecimal system as part of a bargain I strike with everybody else. And, indeed, if we compare end points and ignore the middle range, this is MPD, isn't it?

Complementarity

Now invert the curves, as in Figure 22. Here again there are at least three species. This time, instead of compatibility, we have complementarity. Things are better if people distribute themselves between the choices. But though everyone prefers that the universe be mixed in its choice, he himself may prefer to be in the majority, may prefer to be in the minority, or may have an unconditional preference.

An obvious binary division with complementarity is sex. Let us conjecture, along the lines of Chapter 6, that it becomes possible to choose in advance the sex of one's child. The choice is not binary, since most parents have more than one child and can choose among a few integer mixtures for each family size. But this analysis is only suggestive, so pretend that a family commits itself to boys or to girls.

It is easy to suppose that most prefer the population to be mixed, and probably close to fifty-fifty. But a parent couple could plausibly have any one of three preferences.

First, there might be a uniform preference, everybody

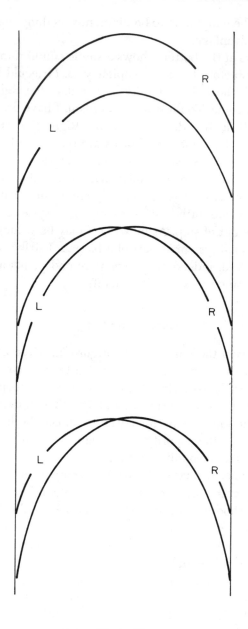

Figure 22

wanting a girl or everybody wanting a boy independently of the sex ratio in the population, while badly wanting that population ratio close to fifty-fifty. Second, everybody might prefer to have a child of the scarcer sex: for dating, marriage, and remarriage, a child of the scarcer sex might be advantaged. Third, the dominant sex might have a majority advantage outweighting "scarcity value," and parents might deplore a preponderance of males or females while electing a child of the preponderant sex.

In one case, there is a happy equilibrium. In one case, there are two unhappy equilibria. And in one case, there is a single unhappy one.

In the unhappy case at the top, we can identify k, the minimum coalition that gains from enforceable contract.

The real problem, if technology should offer the choice and thus create the problem, is attenuated by the nonbinary character of the choice for couples that end up with more than one child. But even the binary illustration is a vivid reminder that a good organizational remedy for severely nonoptimal individual choices is simply not to have the choice—to be victims (beneficiaries) of randomization—and thus to need no organization.

Sufficiency

Turn now to Figure 23. A Right curve cuts a Left straight line twice. Everybody prefers that everybody else choose Right, and over an intermediate range people are induced to choose Right. An example might be the use of insecticides locally: you benefit from the use of insecticides by others; the value of your own insecticides is dissipated unless some neighbors use insecticides, too; with moderate usage by others, it becomes cost-effective to apply your own; and, finally, if nearly everybody uses insecticides, there are not enough bugs to warrant spending your own money.

Communication systems sometimes have that property. If

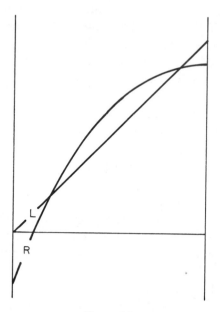

Figure 23

hardly anyone has citizen's-band radio, there is nobody to talk
to; the externality benefits more the people who have sets than
those who do not, though the latter get some benefits from the
communication system; if enough people have sets, others are
induced to procure them as a nearly universal means of communication; finally, if everybody else has a set, you can save
yourself the expense by dropping in on a friend and using his
equipment or handing an emergency message to any passerby,
who will transmit it for you.

A more familiar example is the committee meeting. Everybody suffers if nobody goes; it is not worth going unless there
is likely to be a quorum; over some numerical range, one's
presence makes enough difference to make attendance worthwhile; and if the meeting is large enough, there is no need to
give up the afternoon just to attend.

With these payoff curves, there are two equilibria, one at

the upper-right intersection and one at the left extremity. (If we relabel the curves—and change the interpretation—the equilibria are at the lower-left intersection and the right extremity.)

A Schematic Summary

It is tempting to work out an exhaustive schematic classification for the various possible binary-choice payoff configurations. But the possibilities, though not endless, are many. The curves, even if monotonic, can be concave or convex, S-shaped, flanged or tapered; and, of course, they need not be monotonic. The shapes that are worth distinguishing depend on what we want to single out for analysis—the number of equilibria, the efficiency of equilibria, the role of information or misinformation, the sizes of potential coalitions, the importance of discipline or enforceable contract, the importance of population size and other things. And still we are dealing exclusively with uniform payoffs throughout the population. No logical classification scheme is likely, therefore, to serve everybody's purpose.

But with straight lines the number of distinct situations must be limited—at least, the number that are interestingly different. Still, there are at least the following different situations worth distinguishing:

I. There is a unique equilibrium, with all making the same choice.
  A. It is everybody's favorite outcome.
  B. Everybody would be better off if all made the opposite choice.
    1. The collective total would then be at its maximum.
    2. The collective total would be still larger if only some, not all, made that opposite choice, some then faring better than others but all better than at the equilibrium.
  C. The collective total would be larger if some, not all, made the opposite choice, but some would then be worse off than at the equilibrium.

II. There is a unique equilibrium with some choosing L, some R.
  A. All would be better off if all chose R.
    1. The collective total would then be a maximum.
    2. The collective total would be even higher if some still chose L, everybody still being better off than at the equilibrium, but not equally so.
  B. The collective total would be higher, although some people would be worse off, if some (not all) choosing L chose R instead.
  C. The collective total is at a maximum.

III. There are two equilibria, each with all making the same choice.
  A. One of them is everybody's favorite outcome.
    1. The lesser equilibrium, however, is better than most mixtures of choices.
    2. The lesser equilibrium is worse than most or all mixtures of choices.
  B. The two equilibria are equally satisfactory and superior to all mixtures of choices.

These several cases can be illustrated in the figures already presented. Case I A is represented by Figure 14 A if we relabel the L and R curves, a unanimous choice of R then providing the highest value available. Case I B 1 is then Figure 14 A as drawn, or 14 C; I B 2 corresponds to Figure 14 B. And I C is depicted in Figure 18. Case II A, both 1 and 2, are illustrated by Figure 15, depending on the steepness of the R curve; II B is Figure 17 and II C would be the special case of Figure 17 if we rotate one of the lines until the maximum coincides with the intersection. Case III A 1 would be depicted by Figure 17 if we relabel the L and R curves (or, alternatively, rotate the L curve in Figure 16 about the intersection until it slopes up to the left instead). III A 2 is Figure 16, and III B would be III A 1 if the L curve were as high on the left as the R curve on the right.

With curvature rather than straight lines the variety increases; we can have, as in the lower part of Figure 22, two inferior equilibria, and so on.

In every case, the term "equilibrium" should be qualified to read "potential equilibrium." The order and timing of choices and the reversibility of choices; information about others' choices; signaling, bargaining and organizing processes; custom, precedent, and imitation; and many other crucial elements have been left unspecified. So we have no assurance that actual choices would converge stably on what we have identified as a "potential equilibrium."

For that reason, this is not a classification of binary-choice *situations*, which may differ as importantly in those other characteristics as in their payoffs, but refers only to the shapes of the binary-choice outcome curves.

Index